Auditions and Scenes from Shakespeare

Auditions and Scenes from Shakespeare

is published by **Theatre Directories** in Dorset, Vermont

Theatre Directories, Jill Charles, Editor, is a project of American Theatre Works, Inc., a non-profit educational and cultural organization.

Theatre Directories
P.O. Box 519, Dorset, VT 05251
Phone: (802) 867-2223 FAX: 802-867-0144

Library of Congress Catalogue Card Number: 79-54914
ISBN: 0-933919-27-1

Auditions and Scenes from Shakespeare

by
Richard O. Bell
& Joan Kuder Bell

About the Authors:

Richard and Joan Bell are directors of and actors with The Upstart Crow, a classical ensemble theatre company in Boulder, Colorado. They are currently involved in reconstructing First Folio texts of Shakespeare as actors' and directors' scripts.

Other Publications from Theatre Directories:

Regional Theatre Directory
   Jobs & Internships at 430 Regional & Dinner Theatres

Summer Theatre Directory
   475 Summer Theatres & Summer Training Programs

Directory of Theatre Training Programs
   Programs at 400 Colleges, Universities, & Conservatories

The Actor's Picture/Resume Book
   by Jill Charles with theatrical photographer Tom Bloom

Showbiz Bookkeeper
   Tax Record-Keeping System for Professionals in the Arts

For more information or to order books:
Theatre Directories
P.O. Box 519, Dorset, VT 05251
☎ (802) 867-2223; © 802-867-0144

TABLE OF CONTENTS

Introduction _____ i

How to Use This Book _____ iii

Women's Monologues _____ 1

Men's Monologues _____ 19

Scenes for Two Men _____ 64

Scenes for Two Women _____ 87

Scenes for One Man and One Woman _____ 91

Scenes for Three Actors _____ 107

Scenes for Four and Five Actors _____ 120

INDEX

Women's Monologues, by Time _____ 131

Men's Monologues, by Time _____ 134

Scenes, by Time _____ 140

All Pieces, by Play Title _____ 147

All Characters, by Age Range_____ 159

Specialty Scenes _____ 163

The Plays of Shakespeare _____ 164

To John and Lilia Busby,
"the onlie begetters."

INTRODUCTION

Auditions and Scenes from Shakespeare is a comprehensive listing of speeches and scenes from Shakespeare's plays for the use of actors, directors and teachers. This book is a directory, not an anthology. It contains references to the scenes and descriptions of them, not the scenes themselves. It is, therefore, far more comprehensive than an anthology of a similar size could be. It is based on a perusal of the entire Shakespearean dramatic canon, including *The Two Noble Kinsmen* and the extant fragment of *Sir Thomas More*.

It contains over seven hundred listings. That number, in the opinion of the editors, represents everything in Shakespeare that meets the normal requirements of monologue or scene work. We have included every existing scene for up to five actors in which the sizes of the roles are approximately equal and no actor has less than a minute's worth of material. Thus, the shortest monologues are about a minute long; the shortest five-actor scenes, about five minutes long.

There are, of course, performance situations where such considerations are unnecessary. The producer or company that wishes to do a Shakespearean scene and has available any number of actors of varying abilities, does not need this book. Such a producer or company simply finds a scene to his or its liking, and then casts leads, bits, and walk-ons as needed. *Auditions and Scenes from Shakespeare* is intended as a help for performers who find themselves in the more usual—and more frustrating—situations. For instance:

- The actor who is preparing an audition for a play or a company;
- The student actor, who, with one or more colleagues, has been told to prepare a scene of a certain length, and
- The teacher who is making such an assignment.

Under these circumstances there is rarely time for a thorough search for material. Actors depend on their memories or those of their friends. Those with limited knowledge of Shakespeare engage in random hunts through the pages of the few plays they know a little about. Teachers, consulted by desperate students, recommend the last scene they have watched in a class. The result is still another performance of Petruchio's first meeting with Katharina or the balcony scene, or "Friends, Romans, countrymen." These may be excellent passages—and they are in this book—but they are tired old chestnuts. There is equally good material in such neglected plays as *Henry VI, Part I; The Two Noble Kinsmen,* and *Pericles.*

Auditions and Scenes from Shakespeare should make the search for performance material easier and should call attention to some excellent, but ignored passages. It should be pointed out that this is not a guide to the beauties of Shakespeare. We have included passages because they are actable, not because they are purple. The aesthetic judgements are finally up to the user.

— Richard O. Bell and Joan Kuder Bell
Boulder, Colorado, 1994

HOW TO USE THIS BOOK

ORGANIZATION

The book is divided into the following chapters: Women's Monologues; Men's Monologues; Scenes for Two Men; Scenes for Two Women; Scenes for One Man and One Woman; Scenes for Three Actors; and finally, Scenes for Four and Five Actors. Each selection is set off with a boldface heading showing the play, character(s) and length of the piece. Within each chapter, the ordering is alphebetized by character name in the monologue chapters, and by play title in the scene chapters.

TIME

The number in the right margin of the heading of each selection is the length of the scene. We have assumed a speaking rate of twenty lines per minute, made allowances for cuts, tetrameter passages, and other short lines, and divided to arrive at the length.

Twenty lines per minute is a rapid rate for almost all actors and listeners. All the scenes will play longer than the nominal time we have assigned them. Obviously, it is easier to shorten a scene than to lengthen one, so we have chosen to err in favor of underestimating the time. If a group of actors is looking for a five-minute scene, they can be assured that every scene marked 5:00 (or longer) contains at least five minutes of usable material. They can then shorten the scene according to their own performance speed.

CHESTNUTS

The symbol ✗ which appears after the time in some selections indicates a scene that in our opinion is a chestnut. There is nothing intrinsically wrong with scenes so marked. Most of them are deservedly famous—they range among Shakespeare's most beautiful passages. But the actor should be warned that when he performs one of these, his teacher or director or audience has probably seen it before. Is there anyone who has not heard Hamlet's third soliloquy (p. 37) or Romeo and Juliet's balcony scene (p. 104)? It is one of the purposes of this book to direct actors to some relatively unexploited scenes.

REFERENCE TO SCENE

The references to the scenes are in the standard, familiar form: Act, scene, and inclusive line numbers of the scene. We have used the lineation of the Temple Shakespeare. Most editions follow the Temple line numbering even when it does not fit their own page width. Scenes entirely in verse would present no problem, of course, in any edition. If the actor is using a Shakespeare that does not show the Temple lineation, he may have to search a little for prose selections. But since most of our scenes begin and end with entrances and exits, they should be easy enough to find. There is no standard lineation for *The Two Noble Kinsmen* and *Sir Thomas More*, but again, there should be no real difficulty finding scenes in these plays. The shortened titles used in the entries should be clear; if not, consult the list of plays on page 164.

PROSE AND VERSE, MONOLOGUE AND SOLILOQUY

The description of passages as prose or verse is based on the conventional lineation in modern editions. That does not always agree with the setting in the original Quartos and Folios—but the student or auditioner who is asked to do a verse speech ought to be interested in meeting the expectations of his teacher or director, not in making an antiquarian point.

In the men's and women's monologue chapters, assume that the piece is a monologue—that is, a lengthy speech spoken to other characters on stage, or in some cases directed to the audience—unless it is designated *soliloquy*, which indicates that the character is alone on stage.

SYNOPSIS

In the synopsis of each scene which makes up the bulk of the entry, we have attempted to suggest, subject to space limitations, something of the quality of the scene and the special challenges and problems it may present. Some scenes demand skills in fencing, mime or singing; some require the ability to suggest the presence of characters not actually there; and some call for props or weapons. Such things are included in the descriptions. In scenes for three, four and five actors, the names of the speaking characters are in capital letters.

Since this is a book for performers, not spectators, we have included only scenes in which there are respectable roles for all the actors. If there is no mention of the size of the roles in a scene, it can be assumed that all the roles are approximately equal in length. When differences in role length are significant, we have indicated in percentages the sizes of the smallest and the largest roles. Longer scenes tend to be more unbalanced in terms of role length, but longer scenes are also more likely to be cut. If the cuts are made in the larger roles, balance is easily accomplished. Thus, three actors looking for a balanced five-minute scene may find an unbalanced seven- or eight-minute scene which they can edit to their requirements. Actors are urged to look at all entries appropriate to their number and genders that are longer than the minimum length they can use.

EDITING

Many of the scenes we have listed can be played just as they appear in the play; the only editing instructions necessary are the numbers of the first and last lines. But many are not playable as written, usually because they require extra actors with very small roles. In such cases, we have provided (in italics following the synopsis) directions on cutting, combining roles, or reassigning speeches so that every actor has enough to do. In a very few instances, we have suggested actual changes in the language of the speeches, but these changes are minor—the substitution of one personal pronoun for another, for instance.

ROLES FOR WOMEN

As every actress knows, Shakespeare did not write many roles for women. A number of characters, however, though written as male, can be and often are played by women. Puck and Ariel are the two notable examples, but there are also a number of pages, servants, boys, choruses, messengers, doctors, and other characters which are not gender-specific as written. We have entered such monologues and 2-character scenes in each appropriate chapter, with the "breeches part" in brackets. In scenes of three or more characters, we have indicated in the heading an alternative breakdown in brackets, i.e.: 3M [2M, 1W].

INDEXES

We have cross-indexed the entries in a variety of ways to make the book most usable for the actor, student and teacher. Under various circumstances, the determining factor in choosing a selection might be a piece's genre (comedy, tragedy, romance or history); a character's age or type; a scene's length or special requirements. The cross-referencing to be found in the index is meant to make it easy to find a piece appropriate for the given circumstances.

A FINAL NOTE ON USAGE

Users of this book should be aware of an important distinction between the audition process and the acting class. In choosing an audition piece, the actor should look for a role in which he or she would realistically be cast, that is, of an age and physical type appropriate to the actor. Acting classes and scene studies are the place to stretch oneself, and try out characters which may be far from oneself in physical type or age. An "ingenue" might have a ball with Lady Macbeth in an acting class, whereas she would be better advised to look for a speech of Helena's when auditioning for a Shakespeare festival. Likewise, though a young man might be applauded for his courage in taking on Lear for an acting class, he is jeopardizing his chances if he chooses Lear for a professional audition. Choosing an audition piece which is dramatically against type is detrimental in such circumstances, for it indicates to the director that the actor does not have a realistic idea of how he or she would be cast in a professional situation.

WOMEN'S MONOLOGUES
Listed in alphabetical order, by character name.

ADRIANA   *Comedy of Errors*   **1:51**

Act II, sc. ii, lines 112-148 (verse)

Adriana chides Antipholus of Syracuse (the wrong brother) for being unfaithful to her.

ANNE   *Richard III*   **1:36**

Act I, sc. ii, lines 1-32 (verse)

Anne, following the coffin of King Henry VI, pauses: "Set down, set down your honorable load," laments the king's death, and curses his murderer, Gloucester.

ANNE   *Richard III*   **1:24**

Act IV, sc. i, lines 58-87 (verse)

Anne, upon learning she is to be crowned queen, resigns herself to the idea that Richard will be rid of her: "And I in all unwillingness will go."
(Cut Queen Elizabeth's speech and also cut "No! why?" from line 66.)

CLEOPATRA   *Antony & Cleopatra*   **1:09**

Act I, sc. v, lines 1-34 (verse)

Cleopatra is restless during Antony's absence: "Give me to drink mandragora.../That I might sleep out this great gap of time/My Antony is away."
(Incorporate Charmian's line 6 into Cleopatra's speech, changing "you" to "I"; cut rest of Charmian's & Mardian's lines as well as "Hast thou affections" from line 12 and "Indeed!" from line 14.)

CLEOPATRA   *Antony & Cleopatra*   **1:30**

Act IV, sc. xv, lines 59-91 (verse)

Cleopatra's lament over Antony's body: "There is nothing left remarkable/Beneath the visiting moon."

CLEOPATRA   *Antony & Cleopatra*   **1:06**

Act V, sc. ii, lines 76-100 (verse)

Cleopatra's dream of Antony: "His delights were dolphin-like..."
(*Cut Dolabella's lines and Cleopatra's line 95, "You lie..."*)

CLEOPATRA	*Antony & Cleopatra*	1:41 ✗

Act V, sc. ii, lines 238-241, 283-316 (verse)
Cleopatra dies. Difficult scene because she must kiss Iras, who dies from the kiss; also Charmian's presence must be indicated.
(*Cut Charmian's lines as well as Cleopatra's line 303.*)

CONSTANCE	*King John*	3:14

Act III, sc. i, lines 1-74 (verse)
Constance rages over the betrothal of Blanche and Lewis and the peace between England and France, for this will ruin her hopes for her son's, Arthur's, succession: "Here I and Sorrows sit./Here is my throne; bid Kings come bow to it."
(*Cut Constance's lines 40-41, 66 and all Salisbury's and Arthur's lines.*)

CONSTANCE	*King John*	2:12

Act III, sc. i, lines 83-129 (verse)
Constance rails against the politics that have ignored her son's claim to the English throne. She becomes hysterical: "War! War! No peace! Peace is to me a war."
(*Cut King Philip's and Austria's lines.*)

CONSTANCE	*King John*	3:31

Act III, sc. iv, lines 21-105 (verse)
Constance, mad with grief over the capture of her son, Arthur, berates King Philip and Pandulph for betraying him to the English: "Grief fills the room up of my absent child."
(*Cut Pandulph's and Philip's lines, except Philip's line 68, which is given to Constance with a change of pronoun. Cut Constance's lines 37 and 91.*)

CONSTANCE	*King John*	6:45

Act III, sc. i, lines 1-74 and sc. iv, lines 21-105 (verse)
(*For a longer monologue, combine the two selections above.*)

CORDELIA   *King Lear*   0:51

Act IV, sc. vii, lines 26-42 (verse)

Cordelia speaks to the sleeping Lear, pitying his ordeals: "Was this a face/To be opposed against the warring winds?" *(Cut Kent's line 29.)*

DUCHESS of GLOU.   *Richard II*   2:57

Act I, sc. ii, lines 9-74 (verse)

The Duchess begs her brother-in-law, John of Gaunt, to aid her in revenging her husband's death: "Finds brotherhood in thee no sharper spur?" *(Incorporate Gaunt's line 43, "To God, the widow's champion and defence." Cut Gaunt's other lines.)*

DUCHESS of GLOU.   *Henry VI, Part II*   1:54

Act II, sc. iv, lines 19-57 (verse)

The Duchess, forced to do penance for treason, upbraids Gloucester for allowing her to be shamed: "Come you, my lord, to see my open shame?" *(Cut Glouchester's lines.)*

DUCHESS OF YORK   *Richard III*   1:21

Act II, sc. ii, lines 47-88 (verse)

The Duchess laments the deaths of her husband and two sons: "Ah, so much interest have I in thy sorrow/As I had title in thy noble husband!" *(Cut Warwick's, Margaret Plantagent's and Queen Elizabeth's lines.)*

DUCHESS of YORK   *Richard III*   1:18

Act IV, sc. iv, lines 165-195 (verse)

The Duchess of York stops her son, King Richard, on his way to battle and curses him: "Thou camest on earth to make the earth my hell." *(Cut Richard's lines.)*

EMILIA   *Othello*   1:36

Act IV, sc. iii, lines 68-104 (verse)

Emilia admits to Desdemona that she haas no qualms about cuckolding Iago: "The worlds a huge thing. It is a

great price/For a small vice."
Cut Desdemona's lines 70, 78 & 79. Change Desdemona's line 84 to read: "You do not think there is any such woman?"

EMILIA   *Two Noble Kinsmen*   **1:24**

Act I, sc. iii, lines 55-82 (verse)

Emilia, referring to the great friendship between Theseus and Pirithous, tells of a childhood friend of hers and states, "The true love 'tween maid and maid may be/More than in sex dividual."

EMILIA   *Two Noble Kinsmen*   **3:00**

Act IV, sc. ii, lines 1-54, 58-64 (verse, soliloquy)

Emilia, who is to be the prize in a duel to the death between Palamon and Arcite, contemplates their pictures and hopes for success for one and then the other: "What a mere child is Fancy,/That having two fair guards of equal sweetness,/Cannot distinguish, but must cry for both."

EMILIA   *Two Noble Kinsmen*   **1:51**

Act V, sc. i, lines 138-174 (verse)

Emilia, the prize in a combat between Palamon and Arcite, prays to Diana to grant that she be won by the one who loves her best: "O sacred, shadowy, cold and constant Queen,/Abandoner of revels, mute, contemplative."

HELENA   *All's Well*   **1:21**

Act I, sc. iii, lines 197-223 (verse, soliloquy)

Helena admits to the Countess that she loves Bertram but has no hope of winning him: "Then I confess,/Here on my knee, before high heaven and you,/That before you, and next unto high heaven,/I love your son."

HELENA   *Midsummer*   **1:18**

Act I, sc. i, lines 226-251 (verse)

Helena, having lost Demetrius to Hermia, ponders the fickleness of love and hits upon a plan to win Demetrius back. The speech is all in rhymed couplets.

HELENA   *Midsummer*   **3:21**

Act III, sc. ii, lines 145-161, 192-244 (verse)

Helena chides Hermia, Lysander and Demetrius for supposedly making her the butt of their joke: "Ay, do, persever, counterfeit sad looks,/Make mouths upon me when I turn my back;/Wink each at other; hold the sweet jest up:/This sport, well carried, shall be chronicled."
(Cut Hermia's lines.)

HERMIONE　　　*Winter's Tale*　　　**3:53**

Act III, sc. ii, lines 23-55, 62-77, 92-117, 120-124 (verse)

Hermione defends herself in court against the charge of adultery. She speaks simply but powerfully, stating her case and disdaining death, but fearing, however, loss of honor.
(Begin line 62 with "For Polixenes.")

IMOGEN　　　*Cymbeline*　　　**4:26**

Act III, sc. iv, lines 1-103 (verse)

Learning that Pisanio is to kill her because his master, her husband, believes her unfaithful, Imogen denies the charge and entreats Pisanio to carry out the deed.
(Cut Pisanio's lines.)

IMOGEN　　　*Cymbeline*　　　**1:21**

Act III, sc. vi, lines 1-27 (verse, soliloquy)

Imogen, lost, hungry and tired, seeks shelter in a cave: "I see a man's life is a tedious one."

IMOGEN　　　*Cymbeline*　　　**2:06**

Act IV, sc. ii, lines 291-332 (verse)

Imogen awakens from a drugged sleep and discovers the headless body of Cloten, which, by its clothes, she takes to be the body of her husband, Posthumus. She grieves and blames Cloten and Pisanio: "O!/Give color to my pale cheek with thy blood,/That we the horrider may seem to those/Which chance to find us."

JAILER'S DAUGHTER　　　*Two Noble Kinsmen*　　　**1:39**

Act II, sc. iii, lines 1-33 (verse)

The Jailer's Daughter, in love with Palamon, her father's prisoner, resolves to set him free to win his love.

JAILER'S DAUGHTER　　　*Two Noble Kinsmen*　　　**1:57**

Act II, sc. v, lines 1-39 (verse, soliloquy)

The Jailer's Daughter has set Palamon free. She describes him, his reluctancwe to escape and her love for him: "To marry him is hopeless;/To be his whore is witless."

JAILER'S DAUGHTER	Two Noble Kinsmen	1:54

Act III, sc. ii, lines 1-38 (verse, soliloquy)

The Jailer's Daughter has set Palamon free and hidden him in the woods. But now, unable to find him again, she despairs, fears that he will be killed (he is still in chains) and fears that she will go mad.

JAILER'S DAUGHTER	Two Noble Kinsmen	1:18

Act III, sc. iv, lines 1-26 (verse)

The Jailer's Daughter, having fallen in love with Palamon, has freed him, hidden him, and lost him. Ophelia-like, she goes mad and sings.

JAILER'S DAUGHTER	Two Noble Kinsmen	1:36

Act IV, sc. iii, lines 9-45 (prose)

The Jailer's Daughter, gone mad from love of Palamon, has a vision of Hell and the punishments of sexual offenders. *(Her lines can be extracted easily from the scene.)*

JAILER'S DAUGHTER	Two Noble Kinsmen	6:48

Act II, scs. iii, v; Act III, scs. ii, iv, and Act IV, iii (verse/prose)
(Combine the four verse soliloquies and a prose monologue, all previously cited, for a longer piece, carrying the Jailer's Daughter from courageous love to guilty insanity. Probably Fletcher, not Shakespeare.)

JOAN LA PUCELLE	Henry VI, Part I	1:42

Act III, sc. iii, lines 41-77 (verse)

Joan convinces Burgundy to change sides and fight for France.
(Cut Burgundy's lines.)

JOAN LA PUCELLE	Henry VI, Part I	1:27

Act V, sc. iii, lines 1-29 (verse)

Joan is deserted by her attending fiends, and sees in this the impending victory of the English. An unconventional view of Joan of Arc.

JULIA   *Two Gentlemen*   1:18 ✗

Act I, sc. ii, lines 104-129 (verse, soliloquy)
  Julia panics after tearing up a love letter from Proteus: "O hateful hands, to tear such loving words!"

JULIA   *Two Gentlemen*   1:21

Act IV, sc. iv, lines 184-210 (verse, soliloquy)
  After meeting Silvia, her rival for Proteus' love, Julia compares herself to Silvia: "A virtuous gentlewoman, mild and beautiful."

JULIET   *Romeo & Juliet*   1:39 ✗

Act III, sc. ii, lines 1-33 (verse, soliloquy)
  Juliet, impatient for the consummation of her marriage to Romeo, urges night to fall: "Gallop apace, you fiery-footed steeds."

JULIET   *Romeo & Juliet*   2:55

Act III, sc. ii, lines 71-137 (verse)
  Juliet learns that Romeo has killed Tybalt and has also been banished: "Oh, serpent heart, hid with a flowering face!/Did ever dragon keep so fair a cave?" She is torn between her love for her cousin and for her new husband. *(Cut the Nurse's lines.)*

JULIET   *Romeo & Juliet*   2:15 ✗

Act IV, sc. iii, lines 14-58 (verse, soliloquy)
  The potion speech: Juliet mistrusts the drug that Friar Laurence gave her but finally drinks it: "O, if I wake, shall I not be distraught,/Environed with all these hideous fears,/And madly play with my forefathers' joints."

KATHARINA   *Taming of the Shrew*   2:12 ✗

Act V, sc. ii, lines 136-179 (verse)
  Katharina's warning to shrewish women: "Fie, fie! Unknit that threatening unkind brow..."

LADY MACBETH	*Macbeth*	2:23 ✗

Act I, sc. v, lines 1-32, 39-55 (verse, soliloquy)

Lady Macbeth contemplates the murder of Duncan: "The raven himself is hoarse/That croaks the fatal entrance of Duncan/Under my battlements."

(The Messenger, whose information is vital, may be eliminated thus: Lady Macbeth carries two letters. She reads the first as indicated in the text and finishes the opening speech. Then she opens the second letter and speaks the Messenger's line, "The King comes here tonight," and proceeds to the second speech: "The raven himself...")

LADY MACBETH	*Macbeth*	1:00 ✗

Act V, sc. i, lines 35-76 (prose)

Lady Macbeth's sleep-walking scene: "Out, damned spot! out, I say!"

(Cut the Doctor's and Gentlewoman's lines.)

LADY PERCY	*Henry IV, Part I*	1:27

Act II, sc. iii, lines 39-67 (verse)

Lady Percy, full of love and concern, asks her husband, Hotspur, why they have not made love for two weeks and why his sleep is so restless.

LADY PERCY	*Henry IV, Part II*	1:51

Act II, sc. iii, lines 9-45 (verse)

Lady Percy urges her father-in-law not to support the rebellion which killed her husband, Hotspur. She argues that Northumberland wrongs Hotspur's ghost if he helps others when he would not help his own son.

LUCIANA	*Comedy of Errors*	1:24

Act III, sc. ii, lines 1-28 (verse)

Luciana mistakes Antipholus of Syracuse for his brother, her brother-in-law, and chides him in rhyming quatrains for being strange with his wife.

MISTRESS QUICKLY	*Henry IV, Part II*	1:18

Act II, sc. i, lines 14-18, 25-45 (prose)

Mistress Quickly grows angrier as she tells Snare and Fang why she wants them to arrest Falstaff.

MISTRESS QUICKLY   *Henry IV, Part II*   1:03

Act II, sc. i, lines 92-112 (prose)

Mistress Quickly pins down the exact moment when Falstaff proposed marriage to her.

MISTRESS QUICKLY   *Henry V*   1:00 ✗

Act II, sc. iii, lines 9-28 (prose)

Mistress Quickly, the Hostess, describes the death of Falstaff: "Nay, sure, he's not in Hell..." Comically structured, but quite poignant.

MISTRESS QUICKLY   *Merry Wives of Windsor*   3:12

Act II, sc. ii, lines 60-136 (prose)

Mistress Quickly lures Falstaff into a plot hatched by Mrs. Ford and Mrs. Page—she says they are both in love with him: "You have brought her into such a canaries as 'tis wonderful."

(Cut Falstaff's lines. Cut Quickly's lines 117-118 and begin that speech with "But Mistress Page...")

NURSE   *Romeo & Juliet*   2:15 ✗

Act I, sc. iii, lines 16-62 (verse)

The Nurse chatters on about the death of her daughter and about how she raised Juliet: "Even or odd, of all days in the year,/Come Lammas Eve at night shall she be fourteen."

(Cut Lady Capulet's and Juliet's lines.)

OPHELIA   *Hamlet*   3:45

Act IV, sc. v, lines 22-73, 164-200 (prose/verse)

Ophelia's mad scene: "I would give you some violets, but they withered all when my father died."

(Cut King's, Queen's, and Laertes' lines. Ophelia must sing.)

PAULINA   *Winter's Tale*   2:39

Act III, sc. ii, lines 174-233 (verse)

Paulina tells Leontes his queen is dead and curses him for being responsible. Then, seeing his grief, she repents what she has said: "Woe the while!/O, cut my lace, lest my heart, cracking it,/Break too!"
(Cut Leontes' and the Lord's speeches.)

| **PHEBE** | *As You Like It* | **1:00** |

Act III, sc. v, lines 8-27 (verse)

Phebe tries to dissuade Silvius from loving her: "I would not be thy executioner."

| **PHEBE** | *As You Like It* | **1:54** |

Act III, sc. v, lines 92-139 (verse)

Phebe mulls over her sudden infatuation with Ganymede: "It is a pretty youth—not very pretty—/But, sure, he's proud, and yet his pride becomes him."
(Cut Silvius' lines. Combine lines 135 and 136: "And thou shalt bear it: I'll write it straight...)

| **PORTIA** | *Julius Caesar* | **2:51 X** |

Act II, sc. i, lines 237-56, 261-78, 280-87, 292-302 (verse)

Portia begs her husband, Brutus, to reveal to her what is troubling him; she argues that, if he won't confide in her, then "Portia is Brutus' harlot, not his wife."
(Cut from Portia's line 237, "Nor for yours neither.")

| **PORTIA** | *Julius Caesar* | **1:09** |

Act II, sc. iv, lines 1-46 (verse)

Brutus' wife, Portia, is paralyzed with inaction because of her fears concerning Brutus.
(Cut Lucius' and the Soothsayer's lines.)

| **PORTIA** | *Merchant of Venice* | **1:12** |

Act III, sc. ii, lines 1-24 (verse)

Portia tells Bassanio that she is loathe to have him choose a casket immediately because, if he chooses the wrong one, he must never see her again.

| **PORTIA** | *Merchant of Venice* | **1:09** |

Act III, sc. ii, lines 40-62 (verse)

Portia asks for music to play while Bassanio decides which casket will give her to him as a bride.

PORTIA	*Merchant of Venice*	2:21

Act III, sc. ii, lines 1-24, 40-62
(For a longer monologue, combine the two selections above.)

PORTIA	*Merchant of Venice*	1:06 ✗

Act IV, sc. i, lines 184-205 (verse)
  "The quality of mercy is not strained..."

QUEEN	*Richard II*	1:13

Act V, sc. i, lines 1-34 (verse)
  Richard's Queen bids him farewell as he goes to his internment: "What, is my Richard both in shape and mind/Transformed and weakened?"
(Cut Richard's speech.)

QUEEN ELIZABETH	*Richard III*	1:00

Act IV, sc. iv, lines 377-396 (verse)
  Queen Elizabeth asks Richard to swear by something he hasn't profaned: "God's wrong is most of all."
(Include Richard's line 387 as part of the speech, changing it to a question.)

QUEEN KATHARINE	*Henry VIII*	2:15

Act II, sc. iv, lines 13-57 (verse)
  Kneeling before Henry VIII, Queen Katharine pleads the legality of their marriage.

QUEEN KATHARINE	*Henry VIII*	1:06

Act II, sc. iv, lines 68-84, 105-121 (verse)
  Queen Katharine rejects Cardinal Wolsey as her judge at the trial regarding the legality of her marriage to King Henry, calling him her enemy.
(Cut Cardinal Wolsey's lines; cut Katharine's line 74 and first half of line 75.)

QUEEN KATHARINE	*Henry VIII*	3:49

Act II, sc. iv, lines 13-57, 68-73, 75-84, 105-121 (verse)

Kneeling before Henry VIII, Queen Katharine pleads the legality of their marriage. She then confronts Wolsey and accuses him of conspiring against her: "Sir,/I am about to weep; but...my drops of tears/I'll turn to sparks of fire."

(Combines the two previous selections. Cut Wolsey's line 69; cut "Or God will punish me" in line 75.)

QUEEN KATHARINE	*Henry VIII*	3:47

Act III, sc. i, lines 68-184 (verse)

Queen Katharine rebuffs Cardinal Wolsey's attempts to make her submit to her trial for divorce: "Ye turn me into nothing..."

(Cut all of Wolsey's and Campeius' lines and Queen Katharine's lines 83, first half of 84, 92, 98-101, first half of 102, and 139-142.

QUEEN KATHARINE	*Henry VIII*	2:12

Act IV, sc. ii, lines 129-173 (verse)

Katharine bids an ambassador from Charles V deliver a letter, her will, to Henry VIII. Then she bids farewell to her servants: "Strew me over/With maiden flowers, that all the world may know/I was a chaste wife to my grave."

(Cut Capucius' lines.)

QUEEN MARGARET	*Henry VI, Part II*	2:00

Act I, sc. iii, lines 45-90 (verse)

Queen Margaret complains of King Henry's weakness and declares her hatred for the Duchess of Gloucester: "She sweeps it through the Court with troops of ladies,/More like an empress than Duke Humphrey's wife."

(Cut Suffolk's speeches.)

QUEEN MARGARET	*Henry VI, Part II*	1:54

Act III, sc. i, lines 4-41 (verse)

Queen Margaret remarks on the sudden personality change in Humphrey, Duke of Gloucester, since his wife's banishment. She cautions that he is next in line to the throne and may be plotting to depose Henry: "Can you not see? Or will ye not observe/The strangeness of his altered countenance?"

QUEEN MARGARET   *Henry VI, Part II*   3:15

Act III, sc. ii, lines 56-71, 73-121 (verse)

Queen Margaret defends Suffolk and then complains that Henry doesn't love her when he turns away from her: "Why do you rate my Lord of Suffolk thus?" and "Be woe for me, more wretched than he is."

QUEEN MARGARET   *Henry VI, Part II*   1:45

Act III, sc. ii, lines 329-32, 339-56, 380-87, 403-07 (verse)

Queen Margaret bids a tearful farewell to the exiled Suffolk, promising to work to lift the sentence of exile or to join him.

(Four speeches of a dialogue; the actress must suggest the presence and responses of Suffolk.)

QUEEN MARGARET   *Henry VI, Part III*   1:21

Act 1, sc. i, lines 230-256 (verse)

Queen Margaret divorces herself from Henry's bed and table until her son is reinstated as heir to the throne: "Enforced thee! art thou King and wilt be forced?"

QUEEN MARGARET   *Henry VI, Part III*   2:09

Act I, sc. iv, lines 66-108 (verse)

Queen Margaret mocks the captive York by placing a paper crown on his head: "Stamp, rave, and fret, that I may sing and dance."

QUEEN MARGARET   *Henry VI, Part III*   1:54

Act V, sc. iv, lines 1-38 (verse)

Queen Margaret rallies her forces during a losing battle at Tewksbury: "Great lords, wise men ne'er sit and wail their loss,/But cheerly seek how to redress their harms."

QUEEN MARGARET   *Henry IV, Part III*   0:51

Act V, sc.v, lines 51-67 (verse)

Queen Margaret wails over the body of her child, Prince Edward: "O Ned, sweet Ned! Speak to thy mother, boy!"

QUEEN MARGARET   *Richard III*   1:21

Act I, sc. iii, lines 188-214 (verse)

Queen Margaret berates four lords for mourning
Rutland's murder more than the bloody fall of the House of
Lancaster: "What! were you snarling all before I came,/
Ready to catch each other by the throat,/And turn you all
your hatred now on me?"

QUEEN MARGARET   *Richard III*   0:54

Act I, sc. iii, lines 216-234 (verse)

Queen Margaret hurls invectives at Gloucester: "And
leave out thee? Stay, dog, for thou shalt hear me."
(Cut Gloucester's line 234; end with Margaret's "Richard!")

QUEEN MARGARET   *Richard III*   2:51

Act I, sc. iii, lines 157-63, 170-73, 188-214, 216-34 (verse)

Queen Margaret interrupts a gathering of triumphant
Yorkists, quarreling among themselves, and curses all of
them, foreshadowing the rest of the play.
*(A combination of two previously cited speeches and others. The
presence of several characters must be suggested by the actress.)*

QUEEN MARGARET   *Richard III*   2:00

Act IV, sc. iv, lines 35-78 (verse)

Queen Margaret lists the crimes King Richard has
committed against her family: "If ancient sorrow be most
reverend,/Give mine the benefit of seniory,/And let my
woes frown on the upper hand." She gloats over the crimes
Richard has committed against his own family.
(Cut the Duchess of York's lines.)

QUEEN MARGARET   *Richard III*   2:03

Act IV, sc. iv, lines 82-125 (verse)

Queen Margaret takes her revenge on Queen Elizabeth: "I
called thee then vain flourish of my fortune;/I called thee
then poor shadow, painted Queen...
(Cut Queen Elizabeth's lines.)

QUEEN MARGARET *Richard III* 4:03

Act IV, sc. iv, lines 35-78, 82-125 (verse)
(For a longer monologue, combine the two selections above.)

ROSALIND *As You Like It* 2:24

Act III, sc. ii, lines 387-402, 420-453 (prose)
Disguised as Ganymede, Rosalind tells Orlando about her cure for love: "Love is merely a madness, and I tell you deserves as well a dark house and a whip as madmen do."
(Change and incorporate Orlando's line 391 to "His marks were..." and change Rosalind's line 427 to "Yes, I cured one, and in this manner." Cut the rest of Orlando's lines.)

ROSALIND *As You Like It* 1:27 ✗

Act III, sc. v, lines 35-63 (verse)
Rosalind tells Phebe to be less vain and to accept Silvius: "Sell when you can: you are not for all markets."

ROSALIND *As You Like It* 2:48

Act IV, sc. iii, lines 13-75 (verse)
Rosalind is disgusted with Phebe and Silvius. She reads Phebe's 'love' letter to her: "She Phebes me. Mark how the tyrant writes."
(Cut Silvius' and Celia's lines.)

ROSALIND *As You Like It* 1:48

Act V, sc. ii, lines 32-45, 56-74, 78-81 (prose)
Rosalind tells how Oliver and Celia loved at first sight and how they will wed tomorrow along with Rosalind and Orlando: "They are in the very wrath of love and they will together, clubs cannot part them."
(Begin line 78 with "Therefore, put you in your best array."

ROSALIND *As You Like It* 1:12

Epilogue, lines 1-24 (verse)
Rosalind ends the play by enjoining the audience "to like as much of this play as please you."

TITANIA	*Midsummer*	**1:51**

Act II, sc. i, lines 81-117 (verse)

Titania, queen of the fairies, recounts the upheavals in the weather due to the fight between herself and Oberon: "Therefore the winds, piping to us in vain,/As in revenge, have suck'd up from the sea/Contagious fogs..."

VIOLA	*Twelfth Night*	**0:58 ✗**

Act I, sc. v, lines 269-295 (verse)

Viola woos Olivia for Orsino: "Make me a willow cabin at your gate..."
(Cut Olivia's lines except 273, which changes to read "He loves you," and line 286, which changes to read, "I would.")

VIOLA	*Twelfth Night*	**1:15 ✗**

Act II, sc. ii, lines 18-42 (verse, soliloquy)

Viola discovers that Olivia has been fooled by her boy's clothes and has fallen in love with her: "I left no ring with her: what means this lady?/Fortune forbid my outside have not charmed her."

VOLUMNIA	*Coriolanus*	**2:49**

Act III, sc. ii, lines 16-23, 28-31, 39-92 (verse)

Volumnia exhorts her son, Coriolanus, to flatter the people so that he may be named consul: "O sir, sir, sir,/I would have had you put your power well on/Before you had worn it out."
(Cut Coriolanus' and Menenius' lines.)

VOLUMNIA	*Coriolanus*	**4:23**

Act V, sc. iii, lines 87-91, 94-125, 131-182 (verse)

Volumnia pleads with her son, Coriolanus, to spare Rome: "I am hushed until our city be afire,/And then I'll speak a little."

Following are some suggestions for monologues written for male characters that could be played by women:

[BOY]	Henry V	1:27

Act III, sc. ii, lines 29-57 (prose, soliloquy)

    The Boy disapproves of the cowardice and thievery of Pistol, Nym and Bardolph and decides he "must leave them, and seek some better service."

[CHORUS]	Henry V	1:42 ✗

Act I, Prologue, lines 1-34 (verse, soliloquy)

    The Chorus begs indulgence for the limitations of "this wooden O," the Globe Theatre: "O for a muse of fire."

[CHORUS]	Henry V	2:06

Act II, Prologue, lines 1-42 (verse, soliloquy)

    "Now all the youth of England are on fire."

[CHORUS]	Henry V	1:45

Act III, Prologue, lines 1-35 (verse)

    "Thus with imagined wing our swift scene flies/ In motion of no less celerity/Than that of thought."

[CHORUS]	Henry V	2:39

Act IV, Prologue, lines 1-53 (verse)

    "Now entertain conjecture of a time/When creeping murmurs and the poring dark/Fills the wide vessel of the universe."

[CHORUS]	Henry V	2:15

Act V, Prologue, lines 1-45 (verse)

    "Vouchsafe to those that have not read the story,/That I may prompt them."

[EPILOGUE]	Henry IV, Part II	1:51

Epilogue, lines 1-37

    The Epilogue is delivered by a dancer who begs the audience's pardon for the play. She offers to dance for those who won't accept her apology.

[FIRST PLAYER]	*Hamlet*	**2:56**

Act II, sc. ii, lines 474-541 (verse, soliloquy)

The First Player recites "Aeneas' tale to Dido," about the slaughter of Priam. A difficult speech,deliberately over-written, theatrical, in the manner of Marlowe. The actress must act an actor acting.

(Include Hamlet's lines 473, etc. that begin the speech; cut the various interruptions by Plolnius and Hamlet. This speech is technically a monologue,but is delivered as a soliloquy.)

[PIRITHOUS]	*Two Noble Kinsmen*	**1:48**

Act V, sc. iv, lines 48-84 (verse)

Pirithous describes the death of Arcite, how his horse reared and crushed him. Excellent descriptive verse.

[PROLOGUE]	*Henry VIII*	**1:36**

Prologue, lines 1-32 (verse, soliloquy)

"I come no more to make you laugh."

(Rhymed couplets.)

[PUCK]	*Midsummer*	**1:26**

Act V, sc. i, lines 378-397, 430-445 (verse)

Puck describes night as the fairy's day and begs a farewell of the audience.

Speech is in rhyming trochaic tetrameter.

[RUMOUR]	*Henry IV, Part II*	**2:00**

Induction, lines 1-40 (verse, soliloquy)

Rumour provides the history necessary for the audience to understand *Henry IV, Part II.*

MEN'S MONOLOGUES

Listed in alphabetical order, by character name.

AARON	*Titus Andronicus*	1:09

Act II, sc. i, lines 1-25 (verse, soliloquy)

Aaron describes Tamora's ascendancey and his own plans "to wanton with this queen," and profit by it.

ADAM	*As You Like It*	2:39

Act II, sc. iii, lines 2-15, 16-28, 38-55, 69-76 (verse)

Adam warns Orlando that his brother means to kill him and that he must flee: "Master, go on and I will follow thee/To the last gasp, with truth and loyalty."
(Cut "But do not so" in line 38.)

AENEAS	*Troilus & Cressida*	1:22

Act I, sc. iii, lines 256-283 (verse)

Aeneas challenges any of the Greeks to single combat with Hector: "The Grecian dames are sunburnt and not worth/The splinter of a lance."

AGAMEMNON	*Troilus & Cressida*	1:28

Act I, sc. iii, lines 1-30 (verse)

Agamemnon urges the Greek princes to renew their hope of winning the siege of Troy: "Princes,/What grief hath set the jaundice on your cheeks?"

ANGELO	*Measure for Measure*	1:16

Act II, sc. ii, lines 162-187 (verse, soliloquy)

Angelo agonizes over his lust for Isabell: "What's this, what's this? Is it her fault or mine?"

ANTIGONUS	*Winter's Tale*	2:09

Act III, sc. iii, lines 15-58 (verse, soliloquy)

Antigonus reluctantly abandons the infant, Perdita, on a rough sea-coast, and tells of his dream of the baby's mother speaking to him about the deed. Some good pathos.

ANTIPHOLUS of S.   *Comedy of Errors*   1:12
Act III, sc. ii, lines 29-52 (verse)
    Antipholus of Syracuse, mistaken by his sister-in-law for his brother, is confused by her chiding and propositions her in rhyming quatrains.

ANTONY   *Antony & Cleopatra*   1:12
Act III, sc. xi, lines 1-24 (verse)
    Antony's shame at fleeing and losing the Battle of Actium.
(Cut line tagged "All.")

ANTONY   *Julius Caesar*   2:09
Act III, sc. i, lines 148-163, 184-210 (verse)
    Antony makes peace with the conspirators over the body of Caesar after lamenting the assassination: "O, mighty Caesar, dost thou lie so low?"

ANTONY   *Julius Caesar*   1:06 ✗
Act III, sc. i, lines 254-275 (verse, soliloquy)
    Antony's soliloquy over Caesar's corpse: "O pardon me, thou bleeding peice of earth..."

ANTONY   *Julius Caesar*   1:45 ✗
Act III, sc. ii, lines 78-112 (verse)
    Antony's funeral oration: "Friends, Romans, countrymen, lend me your ears."

ANTONY   *Julius Caesar*   8:00 ✗
Act III, sc. ii, lines 78-266 (verse)
    A longer version of Marc Antony's funeral oration over the body of Caesar: "Friends, Romans, countrymen..."
(Cut all the Citizens' lines.)

ARAGON   *Merchant of Venice*   3:08
Act II, sc. ix, lines 9-78 (verse)
    The Prince of Aragon, asked to choose among three caskets to win the hand of Portia, chooses wrong and finds:

"What's here? The portrait of a blinking idiot." Includes 16 lines of rhyming trochaic tetrameter.
(*Cut Portia's lines.*)

ARCITE	*Two Noble Kinsmen*	1:45

Act V, sc. i, lines 34-69 (verse)
Arcite, about to fight to the death against his friend and kinsman, Palamon, prays to Mars to grant him victory in battle.

ARMADO	*Love's Labours Lost*	1:03

Act I, sc. ii, lines 1172-192 (prose, soliloquy)
Armado, in love with Jacquenetta, despairs of conquering Love, and resolves to write love poems: "There is no evil angel but Love."

AUFIDIUS	*Coriolanus*	1:33

Act I, sc. x, lines 1-33 (verse)
Aufidius vows to crush Coriolanus by any means he can employ: "Where I find him, were it/At home, upon my brother's guard, even there, / Against the hospitable canon, would I/Wash my fierce hand in's heart."
(*Cut the First Soldier's last two lines; incorporate the rest into Aufidius' part.*)

AUFIDIUS	*Coriolanus*	2:18

Act IV, sc. v, lines 107-153 (verse)
Aufidius, old enemy of Coriolanus, accepts Coriolanus' offer to fight on his side against Rome.
(*Cut Coriolanus' line 141.*)

BASTARD	*King John*	2:03

Act I, sc. i, lines 180-220 (verse, soliloquy)
Philip the Bastard muses on his new social position now that he has been knighted by King John. Now he can be rude to people.

BASTARD	*King John*	1:54

Act II, sc. i, lines 561-598 (verse, soliloquy)

Philip the Bastard's "commodity" speech that condemns political compromises: "Mad world! Mad Kings! Mad composition!"

BASTARD	King John	1:57

Act V, sc. i, lines 30-36, 44-61, 65-76, 78-79 (verse)
Because he brings news of French victories, Philip the Bastard must rouse King John's morale.
(Cut King John's lines.)

BASTARD	King John	2:15

Act V, sc. ii, lines 127-158, 166-178 (verse)
Philip the Bastard, as King John's envoy, rousingly warns the French that the English will fight. An energetic call-to-arms.

BELARIUS	Cymbeline	4:21

Act II, sc. iii, lines 1-26, 45-107 (verse monologue/soliloquy)
Belarius praises the rustic life and condemns the court to his adopted sons, the true sons of Cymbeline. He sends them off to hunt and tells, in soliloquy, who they and he really are: "How hard it is to hide the sparks of nature."
(Cut the boys' lines.)

BENEDICK	Much Ado	1:57

Act II, sc. i, lines 246-284 (prose)
Benedick defends himself against Beatrice's accusations: "O, she misused me past the endurance of a block!"

BENEDICK	Much Ado	1:36

Act II, sc. iii, lines 7-38 (prose, soliloquy)
Benedick describes the only kind of woman he would marry: "Till all graces be in one woman, one woman shall not come in my grace."

BENEDICK	Much Ado	1:24

Act II, sc. iii, lines 228-255 (prose, soliloquy)
Benedick decides to marry the "lovesick" Beatrice: "This can be no trick..." because "the world must be peopled."

BIRON	*Love's Labours Lost*	1:33

Act III, sc. i, lines 176-207 (verse, soliloquy)

Biron (Berowne) complains of being in love and generally insults women: "And I, forsooth, in love! I, that have been love's whip."

BIRON	*Love's Labours Lost*	3:48

Act IV, sc. iii, lines 290-365 (verse)

Biron (Berowne), in the longest single speech in Shakespeare, reasons himself and his friends out of their vow to avoid women for three years: "Have at you, then, affection's men-at-arms."

BOLINGBROOKE	*Richard II*	1:30

Act III, sc. i, lines 1-30 (verse)

Bolingbrooke enumerates the charges for which Bushy and Green will die.

BOLINGBROOKE	*Richard II*	1:51

Act III, sc. iii, lines 31-67 (verse)

Bolingbrooke sends his lords to King Richard, offering to disband the rebellion if Richard will repeal Bolingbrooke's banishment.

BOY	**Henry V**	1:27

Act III, sc. ii, lines 29-57 (prose, soliloquy)

The Boy disapproves of the cowardice and thievery of Pistol, Nym and Bardolph and decides he "must leave them, and seek some better service."

BRUTUS	**Julius Caesar**	1:21

Act II, sc. i, lines 114-140

Brutus argues against the assassins swearing to their resolution to kill Caesar.

BRUTUS	**Julius Caesar**	1:06

Act II, sc. i, lines 162-183 (verse)

Brutus argues against the assassination of Marc Antony along with Julius Caesar.

BRUTUS   *Julius Caesar*   2:54

Act II, sc. i, lines 10-34, 44-58, 61-69, 77-85 (verse, soliloquy)
    Four of Brutus' soliloquies: "It must be by his death"; "The exhalations whizzing in the air"; "Since Cassius first did whet me against Caesar"; and "They are the faction."

BRUTUS   *Julius Caesar*   2:21

Act III, sc. ii, lines 12-37, 39-52, 60-66 (prose)
    Brutus explains to the citizens why he assassinated Caesar: "Not that I loved Caesar less but that I loved Rome more."

BUCKINGHAM   *Henry VIII*   2:09

Act I, sc. i, lines 150-193 (verse)
    Buckingham vehemently delineates the reasons he feels Cardinal Wolsey should be charged with treason: "To the King I'll say't; and make my vouch as strong/As shore of rock."
(Cut Norfolk's lines.)

BUCKINGHAM   *Henry VIII*   3:35

Act II, sc. i, lines 55-78, 82-94, 101-136 (verse)
    Buckingham forgives his enemies, wishes his king a long life, and asks for his friends' prayers as he goes to his execution: "All good people,/You that thus far have come to pity me,/Hear what I say, and then go home and lose me."

BUCKINGHAM   *Richard III*   1:54

Act III, sc. vii, lines 2-41 (verse)
    Buckingham recounts his failure to incite the Londoners to Gloucester's cause: "Now, by the holy Mother of Our Lord,/The citizens are mum and speak not a word."
(Change l. 5 to read, "I touched on his contract with Lady Lucy..." Cut the "No" in line 24 as well as all of Gloucester's lines.)

BUCKINGHAM   *Richard III*   3:03

Act III, sc. vii, lines 117-140, 177-140, 202, 208-219 (verse)

Buckingham offers Gloucester the English crown: "Then know it is your fault that you resign/The supreme seat, the throne majestical..."

BUCKINGHAM	*Richard III*	1:21

Act V, sc. i, lines 3-30 (verse)
Buckingham's "All-Soul's day" death speech.
(Cut the Sheriff's line.)

BURGUNDY	*Henry V*	2:15

Act V, sc. ii, lines 23-67 (verse)
The Duke of Burgundy encourages Henry V and the French king to work for a desired peace.

CADE	*Henry VI, Part II*	1:15

Act IV, sc. vii, lines 26-50 (prose)
Cade lists the offenses with which he charges Lord Say: "Well, he shall be beheaded for it ten times."
(End with "...when, indeed, only for that cause have they been most worthy to live."

CADE	*Henry VI, Part II*	1:18

Act IV, sc. viii, lines 20-34, 57-67 (prose)
Cade loses the support of the commoners when Clifford offers to pardon them. Cade escapes after they change sides.

CADE	*Henry VI, Part II*	0:51

Act IV, sc. x, lines 1-17 (prose, soliloquy)
Cade, a defeated rebel, on the run and starving, decries his ambition: "Fie on ambition! fie on myself, that have a sword, and yet am ready to famish!"

CAESAR	*Antony & Cleopatra*	1:23

Act V, sc. i, lines 13-49 (verse)
Caesar laments Antony's death.
(Begin with and include Dercetas' "Antony is dead," line 13, include Mecaenas' and Agrippa's lines except lines 33-35, "Caesar is touched...must see himself." Cut Dercetas' lines 19-26.)

CAESAR	*Julius Caesar*	1:03 ✗

Act I, sc. ii, lines 192-195, 198-214 (verse)
"Yond Cassius has a lean and hungry look."

CAESAR	*Julius Caesar*	1:30

Act III, sc. i, lines 35-48, 58-73 (verse)
Caesar refuses to change his mind when Metellus Cimber begs pardon for his banished brother: "But I am constant as the northern star. . ."

CANTERBURY	*Henry V*	3:09

Act I, sc. ii, lines 33-95 (verse)
The Archbishop of Canterbury delivers his "Salique land" speech to convince Henry V to invade France. A convoluted speech by a shrewd politician.

CAPTAIN	*Henry VI, Part II*	1:42

Act IV, sc. i, lines 70-103 (verse)
A pirate Captain passes sentence on Suffolk because of the ills Suffolk has brought to England: "Pool! Sir Pool! lord!/Ay, kennel, puddle, sink; whose filth and dirt . . ."

CARLISLE	*Richard II*	1:48

Act IV, sc. i, lines 114-149 (verse)
The Bishop of Carlisle warns the would-be Henry IV and the lords that the usurpation of King Richard's crown will bring about natural and civil strife: "And if you crown him, let me prophesy,/The blood of English shall manure the ground/And future ages groan for this foul act."

CASCA	*Julius Caesar*	1:36

Act I, sc. ii, lines 236-253, 265-278 (prose)
Casca recounts Marc Antony's offer of a crown to Julius Caesar and Caesar's refusals and his epileptic seizure.

CASCA	*Julius Caesar*	1:27

Act I, sc. iii, lines 3-32 (verse)

Casca comments on the thunderstorm and other unnatural events of the night: "Are not you moved, when all the sway of earth/Shake like a thing unfirm?"
(Cut Cicero's line.)

CASSIUS	*Julius Caesar*	3:27

Act I, sc. ii, lines 90-131, 135-161 (verse)
Cassius recounts Julius Caesar's physical weaknesses in order to point out that there is no reason that the Romans should give up the republic for such a man; Caesar is no greater than Cassius or Brutus: "The fault, dear Brutus, is not in our stars,/But in ourselves. . . "

CASSIUS	*Julius Caesar*	3:30

Act I, sc. iii, lines 45-130 (verse)
Cassius, exhilarated by the storm, reveals to Casca the assassination plot against Caesar: "Cassius from bondage will deliver Cassius."
(Cut Casca's lines.)

CHORUS	*Henry V*	1:42 ✗

Act I, Prologue, lines 1-34 (verse, soliloquy)
The Chorus begs indulgence for the limitations of "this wooden O," the Globe Theatre: "O for a muse of fire..."

CHORUS	*Henry V*	2:06

Act II, Prologue, lines 1-42 (verse, soliloquy)
"Now all the youth of England are on fire."

CHORUS	*Henry V*	1:45

Act III, Prologue, lines 1-35 (verse, soliloquy)
"Thus with imagined wing our swift scene flies/In motion of no less celerity/Than that of thought."

CHORUS	*Henry V*	2:39

Act IV, Prologue, lines 1-53 (verse)
"Now entertain conjecture of a time/When creeping murmurs and the poring dark/Fills the wide vessel of the universe."

CHORUS   *Henry V*   **2:15**

Act V, Prologue, lines 1-45 (verse, soliloquy)

"Vouchsafe to those that have not read the story,/That I may prompt them."

CLARENCE   *Henry VI, Part III*   **1:06**

Act V, sc. i, lines 81-102 (verse)

Clarence, throwing the red rose from his hat at Warwick, returns to the Yorkist side: "Father of Warwick, know you what this means?"

CLARENCE   *Richard III*   **3:17**

Act I, sc. iv, lines 2-74 (verse)

Clarence recounts his nightmare about his death: "O, I have pass'd a miserable night."

(Cut "Methought I had" from line 36 and cut Brakenbury's lines.)

CLAUDIO   *Measure for Measure*   **1:51**

Act III, sc. i, lines 5-41 (verse)

The Duke tells Claudio to prepare for death and describes the ills of life to make him welcome death: "Thou hast nor youth nor age,/But, as it were, an after-dinner's sleep, Dreaming on both."

CLAUDIUS   *Hamlet*   **1:54 ✗**

III, iii, 36-72,97-98 (verse, soliloquy)

Claudius' prayer: "O, my offense is rank, it smells to heaven."

CLIFFORD   *Henry VI, Part II*   **1:45**

Act V, sc. ii, lines 31-65 (verse)

As he told his dead father on the battlefield of St. Alban's, Young Clifford swears to spare no Yorkist: "Shame and confusion! all is on the rout."

CLIFFORD   *Henry VI, Part III*   **1:42**

Act II, sc. ii, lines 9-42 (verse)

Clifford chides King Henry for regretting York's death: "My gracious liege, this is too much lenity."

CLIFFORD	*Henry VI, Part III*	1:30

Act II, sc. vi, lines 1-30 (verse, soliloquy)

Clifford dies with regrets: "Here burns my candle out; ay, here it dies/Which, while it lasted, gave King Henry light."

CLOTEN	*Cymbeline*	1:24

Act IV, sc. i, lines 1-28 (prose, soliloquy)

Cloten tells of his plan to rape Imogen and kill Posthumus. He complains that she does not love him.

COMINIUS	*Coriolanus*	2:18

Act II, sc. ii, lines 86-133 (verse)

Cominius nominates Coriolanus for the consulship by praising his military exploits.

(Cut Menenius' and the First Senator's lines.)

CONSTABLE of FR.	*Henry V*	1:09

Act IV, sc. ii, lines 15-37 (verse)

The Constable of France rallies the French lords to battle at Agincourt: "To horse, you gallant princes! straight to horse!"

CORIOLANUS	*Coriolanus*	1:45

Act IV, sc. i, lines 1-11, 14-33, 48-53 (verse)

Coriolanus, banished by the people, says farewell to his mother and his friends: "A brief farewell. The beast/With many heads butts me away."

CORIOLANUS	*Coriolanus*	1:51

Act IV, sc. v, lines 71-107 (verse)

Coriolanus, banished, offers his services to his old enemy, Aufidius.

CRANMER	*Henry VIII*	1:27

Act V, sc. iii, lines 32-48, 58-69 (verse)

Cranmer's defense of himself against the charge of heresy; his request to face his accusers: "I see your end;/'Tis my undoing."

CRANMER	*Henry VIII*	2:27

Act V, sc. v, lines 15-63 (verse)

Cranmer praises the infant Elizabeth at her christening: "This royal infant—heaven still move about her!—/Though in her cradle, yet now promises/Upon this land a thousand thousand blessings."

(Cut the King's line.)

DOGBERRY	*Much Ado*	0:45 ✗

Act IV, sc. ii, lines 76-90 (prose)

"O that he were here to write me down an ass!"

DON JOHN	*Much Ado*	1:27

Act III, sc. ii, lines 98-137 (prose)

Don John tells Claudio that Hero is unfaithful and offers to prove it: "Leonato's Hero, your Hero, every man's Hero." *(Extract Don John's lines from the scene: cut the others, but keep line 111, "Disloyal?" as part of Don John's lines.)*

DUKE SENIOR	*As You Like It*	1:09

Act II, sc. i, lines 1-18, 21-25 (verse)

Duke Senior extolls exile in the forest of Arden" "Hath not old custom made this life more sweet/Than that of painted pomp?"

EDGAR	*King Lear*	1:03

Act II, sc. iii, lines 1-21 (verse, soliloquy)

Edgar decides to disguise himself as "Tom o' Bedlam."

EDMUND	*King Lear*	1:06 ✗

Act I, sc. ii, lines 1-22 (verse)

Edmund's defense of illegitimacy: "Now, gods, stand up for bastards."

EDWARD	*Richard III*	1:36

Act II, sc. i, lines 102-133 (verse)

King Edward, mortally ill, is shocked to hear that his brother, Clarence, died because his pardon didn't arrive in time: "Have I a tongue to doom my brother's death, /And shall the same give pardon to a slave?"

ENOBARBUS	*Antony & Cleopatra*	2:18

Act II, sc. ii, lines 196-245 (verse)

Enobarbus describes Cleopatra: "Age cannot wither her, nor custom stale/Her infinite variety."
(Cut Mecaenus' and Agrippa's lines and Enobarbus; line 239, "Never. He will not.")

EPILOGUE	*Henry IV, Part II*	1:51

Epilogue, lines 1-37 (verse)

The Epilogue is delivered by a dancer who begs the audience's pardon for the play. He offers to dance for those who won't accept his apology.

EXETER	*Henry V*	1:51

Act II, sc. iv, lines 76-112 (verse)

Exeter tells the French King to resign his crown and kingdom to Henry V, who will forceably take it if necessary.
(Incorporate the French King's line 96 into Exeter's speech.)

EXETER	*Henry V*	1:18

Act IV, sc. vi, lines 7-32 (verse)

Exeter recounts the grief of the dying York over the Earl of Suffolk's death during the Battle of Agincourt.

FALSTAFF	*Henry IV, Part I*	1:09

Act II, sc. ii, lines 10-32 (prose, soliloquy)

Falstaff, exhausted upon reaching the rendezvous of a plotted robbery, complains of his aches and pains and swears to swear off his friends.

FALSTAFF	*Henry IV, Part I*	1:15

Act III, sc. iii, lines 27-52 (prose)

Falstaff mercilessly teases Bardolph who has a bad case of acne.
(Cut Bardolph's line.)

FALSTAFF	*Henry IV, Part I*	2:03

Act IV, sc. ii, lines 12-52 (prose, soliloquy)
Falstaff tells how he has gathered his sorry army by questionable means: "If I be not ashamed of my soldiers, I am a soused gurnet."

FALSTAFF	*Henry IV, Part I*	0:48 ✗

Act V, sc. i, lines 127-142 (prose, soliloquy)
"Honour pricks me on."

FALSTAFF	*Henry IV, Part I*	1:03 ✗

Act V, sc. iv, lines 111-131 (prose, soliloquy)
"The better part of valor is discretion."

FALSTAFF	*Henry IV, Part II*	2:09

Act I, sc. ii, lines 6-32, 36-51 (prose)
Falstaff abuses Prince Hal and a tailor when they cannot hear him, but abuses his page to his face, and says of himself: "I am not only witty in myself, but the cause that wit is in other men."

FALSTAFF	*Henry IV, Part II*	1:48

Act III, sc. ii, lines 323-358 (prose, soliloquy)
Falstaff thinks about how he will use Justice Shallow to his advantage if he returns from war: "Lord, Lord, how subject we old men are to this vice of lying."

FALSTAFF	*Henry IV, Part II*	2:15

Act IV, sc. iii, lines 92-136 (prose, soliloquy)
Falstaff expostulates on the differences between Prince John, who drinks no wine, and himself and Prince Hal, who drink "fertile sherrie" or sack.

FALSTAFF	*Henry IV, Part II*	1:21

Act V, sc. i, lines 69-95 (prose, soliloquy)

Falstaff, offended by Justice Shallow's lack of character, intends to make a fool of him.

FALSTAFF	*Merry Wives*	3:06

Act III, sc. v, lines 62-66, 71-79, 84-140 (prose)

Falstaff tells Mr. Brook, the disguised Ford, about his attempt to seduce Mrs. Ford which led to him being thrown into a ditch from a laundry basket: "and then, to be stopped in, like a strong distillation, with stinking clothes that fretted in their own grease."

(Cut Ford's lines; cut line 68 and "No Master Brook," from line 71; cut "You shall hear" from line 84. Incorporate line 89, "A buck-basket!", cut "Sir" from line 134 and "Is it" from line 135.)

FIRST PLAYER	*Hamlet*	2:56

Act II, sc. ii, lines 474-541 (verse, soliloquy)

The First Player recites "Aeneas' tale to Dido," about the slaughter of Priam. A difficult speech, deliberately over-written, theatrical, in the manner of Marlowe. The actor must act an actor acting.

(Include Hamlet's lines 473 etc. that begin the speech; cut the various interruptions by Poloius and Hamlet. This speech is technically a monologue but is delivered as a soliloquy.)

FLAVIUS	*Timon of Athens*	1:24

Act IV, sc. ii, lines 22-50 (verse)

Flavius, Timon's steward, says farewell to the servants and bemoans the fact that Timon was ruined by his own goodness.

FORD	*Merry Wives*	1:27

Act II, sc.ii, lines 299-327 (prose, soliloquy)

Ford rages because he thinks he has been cuckolded: "What a damned Epicurean rascal is this! My heart is ready to crack with impatience."

FR. LAURENCE	*Romeo & Juliet*	1:30 ✗

Act II, sc. iii, sc. 1-30 (verse, soliloquy)

Friar Laurence inventories the herbs he has gathered for his pharmacy.

FR. LAURENCE   *Romeo & Juliet*   2:33

Act III, sc. iii, lines 108-158 (verse)

Friar Laurence scolds Romeo for his self-pity. He tells him to enjoy his wedding night with Juliet before he goes into exile and that all will work out right.

FRANCE   *All's Well*   2:33

Act I, sc. ii, lines 19-76 (verse)

The King of France reminisces about Bertram's father and ponders about growing old: "But on us both did haggish age steal on/And wore us out of act."

(Cut Bertram's and both Lords' lines.)

FRIAR FRANCIS   *Much Ado*   1:42

Act IV, sc. i, lines 212-245 (verse)

Friar Francis suggests that the rumor that Hero died when she was accused of inconstancy by Claudio be circulated in order to set events straight.

GARDENER   *Richard II*   2:09

Act III, sc. iv, lines 29-71 (verse)

The gardener compares the state and the king's affairs to the garden he works in.

(Incorporate the Servant's lines: cut line 476, "Hold thy peace;" read line 54 as "They are all dead"; read line 67 as "What, think I then the king shall be deposed?")

GAUNT   *Richard II*   1:54 ✗

Act I, sc. i, lines 31-68 (verse)

As he dies, Gaunt describes England: "This royal throne of kings, this sceptered isle..."

GENTLEMAN   *Henry VIII*   1:39

Act IV, sc. i, lines 62-94 (verse)

The Third Gentleman describes Anne Bullen's coronation.

(Cut the Second Gentleman's line 81.)

GHOST   *Hamlet*   3:59

Act I, sc. v, lines 2-91 (verse)

The Ghost of Hamlet's father exhorts Hamlet to "Revenge his foul and most unnatural murder."
(*Cut Hamlet's lines.*)

GLOUCESTER	*Henry VI, Part II*	1:27

Act I, sc. i, lines 75-103 (verse)
Gloucester rages against England handing over Anjou and Maine to the French in return for Margaret of France as Henry's bride. Gloucester charges that too much English blood won those provinces for them to be given away so casually.

GLOUCESTER	*Henry VI, Part II*	1:30

Act III, sc. i, lines 142-171 (verse)
Gloucester: "Ah, gracious lord, these days are dangerous." He warns the king that the lords who accuse him of treason mean the king no good will.

Note: The character of "Gloucester" in Henry VI, Part III is Richard, named Duke of Gloucester in Henry VI, Part III, then assuming the throne as King Richard III in Act IV of Richard III. For clarity's sake we have listed his speeches under the character name "Gloucester" in Henry VI, Part III, and under "Richard III" in that play—see pages 56-57.

GLOUCESTER	*Henry VI, Part III*	3:36

Act III, sc. ii, lines 124-195 (verse, soliloquy)
Gloucester delineates the obstacles in his way to being crowned king and his determination to overcome them: "Can I do this, and cannot get a crown?"

GLOUCESTER	*Henry VI, Part III*	1:39

Act V, sc. vi, lines 61-93 (verse, soliloquy)
Gloucester gloats over King Henry's death: "I am myself alone."

GOWER	*Pericles*	1:41

Act I, Prologue, lines 1-42 (verse, soliloquy)
Gower, as prologue, introduces the play in rhyming iambic tetrameter.

| HAMLET | *Hamlet* | 1:30 ✗ |

Act I, sc. ii, lines 129-159 (verse, soliloquy)

Hamlet's first soliloquy: "O, that this too, too solid flesh would melt."

| HAMLET | *Hamlet* | 4:24 |

Act II, sc. ii, lines 440-541 (verse/prose)

Hamlet greets the players, asks the First Player to recite "Aeneas' tale to Dido" about the slaughter of Priam, and then quotes the speech himself.

(Cut the First Player's "What speech, my lord?" but incorporate the Player's continuation of the speech into Hamlet's part and edit out the various interruptions. Note, however, that this "hybrid" actually contains as many of the First Player's lines as of Hamlet's, and thus the difficulties noted in the listing for First Player, p.33.)

| HAMLET | *Hamlet* | 2:57 ✗ |

Act II, sc. ii, lines 576-634 (verse, soliloquy)

Hamlet's 2nd soliloquy: "O, what a rogue and peasant slave am I!."

| HAMLET | *Hamlet* | 1:39 ✗ |

Act III, sc. i, lines 56-88 (verse, soliloquy)

Hamlet's third soliloquy: "To be or not to be."
(The greatest chestnut of all.)

| HAMLET | *Hamlet* | 1:40 |

Act III, sc. ii, lines 59-92 (verse)

Hamlet explains to Horatio why Horatio is a just man: "Give me that man/That is not a passion's slave, and I will wear him/In my heart's core, ay, in my heart's heart,/As I do thee." Then, Hamlet asks Horatio to watch the king's face during the play.
(Cut Horatio's line.)

| HAMLET | *Hamlet* | 2:30 ✗ |

Act III, sc. ii, lines 1-50 (prose)

Hamlet's advice to the players: "Speak the speech, I pray you..."
(Cut the 1st Player's lines.)

HAMLET	*Hamlet*	7:33

Act III, sc. iv, lines 34-217 (verse)

The closet scene: Hamlet confronts his mother about the murder of his father. The Ghost appears and saves Gertrude from Hamlet's wrath. Hamlet says he "must to England." The actor must be able to place the Queen, the dead Polonius, and the Ghost.
(Cut the Queen's and the Ghost's speeches.)

HAMLET	*Hamlet*	1:12 ✗

Act III, sc. iii,lines 73-96 (verse)

Hamlet comes on Claudius, praying, and decides not to kill him at that moment: "Now might I do it pat, now he is praying."

HAMLET	*Hamlet*	1:45 ✗

Act IV, sc. iv, lines 32-66 (verse, soliloquy)

Hamlet's fourth soliloquy: "How all occasions do inform against me/And spur my dull revenge."

HAMLET	*Hamlet*	2:00

Act V, sc. i, lines 73-74, 83-126 (prose)

Hamlet muses over the nonchalance of the gravedigger who throws skulls up as he digs a new grave: "Did these bones cost no more the breeding, but to play at loggats with 'em? mine ache to think on't."
(Cut Horatio's and the 1st Clown's lines but change line 124 to read, "Ay,...and of calf-skins too," and incorporate it into Hamlet's speech.)

HASTINGS	*Richard III*	1:15

Act III, sc. iv, lines 82-109 (verse)

Hastings is stunned by the swiftness of Gloucester's wrath and his pronouncement of death: "Woe, woe for England! not a whit for me."
(Cut Ratcliff's and Lovel's speeches.)

HENRY IV	*1 Henry IV, Part I*	**1:39**

Act I, sc. i, lines 1-33 (verse)

Wearily, King Henry declares peace and announces a crusade to Jerusalem.

HENRY IV	*Henry IV, Part II*	**5:48**

Act III, sc. ii, lines 1-17, 29-91, 93-128 (verse)

King Henry chides his son, Prince Hal, about his unruly life and warns him that King Richard was deposed for living in just such a frivolous manner. Henry upbraids Hal for not being like Hotspur.

HENRY IV	*Henry IV, Part II*	**1:33**

Act III, sc. i, lines 1-31 (verse, soliloquy)

King Henry, who has been ill, wearily wonders why his subjects sleep so easily and soundly when he cannot sleep at all: "O Sleep, O gentle Sleep/Nature's soft nurse, how have I frighted thee . . ."

HENRY IV	*Henry IV, Part II*	**1:45**

Act III, sc. i, lines 45-79 (verse)

Weary and ill, King Henry asks,"O God! that one might read the book of fate. . ."

HENRY IV	*Henry IV, Part II*	**3:18**

Act III, sc. i, lines 1-31, 45-79 (verse, monologue/soliloquy)

Combine above cited soliloquy "O Sleep, O gentle Sleep,/Nature's soft nurse, how have I frighted thee..." with monologue "O God! that one might read the book of fate..." for a longer piece.

HENRY IV	*Henry VI, Part II*	**1:15**

Act III, sc. i, lines 198-222 (verse)

Henry bemoans the fact that, though he knows Gloucester is innocent, he's powerless to help him: "Ay, Margaret; my heart is drown'd with grief."

HENRY IV	*Henry IV, Part II*	**1:30**

Act IV, sc. iv, lines 19-48 (verse)

King Henry on his sickbed entreats his son Thomas of Clarence, to stay in his brother, Prince Hal's, good graces.

HENRY IV   *Henry IV, Part II*   1:09

Act IV, sc. iv, lines 60-82 (verse)

On his deathbed, King Henry bitterly rails against what he wrongfully considers Prince Hal's ambition.

HENRY IV   *Henry IV, Part II*   2:09

Act IV, sc. iv, lines 178-220 (verse)

On his deathbed, King Henry counsels his heir, Prince Hal, "to busy giddy minds/With foreign quarrels..." when he becomes king so that Hal will not have the civil strife to deal with that he had.

HENRY IV   *Henry IV, Part II*   2:18

Act IV, sc. v, lines 93-138 (verse)

On his deathbed, King Henry accuses his heir, Prince Hal, of taking his crown before Henry has died. Henry's bitter disappointment in Hal surfaces.

Note: In Henry IV, Part I, and in Part II, until King Henry IV's death, his son, later King Henry V, is called "Prince Hal," and all his speeches from those two plays can be found on pages 52-53. His speeches as King Henry V, from the play Henry V, follow here.

HENRY V   *Henry V*   2:36

Act I, sc. ii, lines 259-310 (verse)

Henry V, who has been offered tennis balls as a trade for French soil claimed by England, declares that this insult will lead to an invasion of France.

(Incorporate Exeter's line in Henry's speech.)

HENRY V   *Henry V*   4:42

Act II, sc. ii, lines 79-144, 166-193 (verse)

Anguished, King Henry sentences three treasonous lords to death: "I will weep for thee,/For this revolt of thine, methinks, is like/Another fall of man." Henry then prepares to go to war in France.

HENRY V	*Henry V*	**1:42 ✗**

Act III, sc. i, lines 1-34 (verse)

    King Henry rallies his troops before they storm Harfleur: "Once more unto the breach, dear friends, once more."

HENRY V	*Henry V*	**2:09**

Act III, sc. iii, lines 1-43 (verse)

    Henry V before the gates of Harfleur delivers an ultimatum to the governor: "Will you yield, and this [slaughter] avoid,/Or guilty in defense, be thus destroyed?"

HENRY V	*Henry V*	**3:34**

Act IV, sc. i, lines 247-301, 306-322 (verse, soliloquy)

    King Henry points out that the only difference between kings and subjects is "ceremony," yet "What infinite heartsease/Must kings neglect that private men enjoy." Then he prays, "O God of battles steel my soldiers' hearts!"

HENRY V	*Henry V*	**1:48**

Act IV, sc. iii, lines 90-125 (verse)

    Henry V refuses to forego the battle at Agincourt by giving himself up to the French for ransom: "I pray thee, bear my former answer back:/Bid them achieve me and then sell my bones."

HENRY V	*Henry V*	**2:24 ✗**

Act IV, sc. iii, lines 20-67 (verse)

    King Henry before the Battle of Agincourt: "This day is called the feast of Crispian."

HENRY V	*Henry V*	**2:06**

Act IV, sc. viii, lines 85-121, 127-131 (verse)

    Henry V learns of the slaughter the English dealt the French at Agincourt and recommends that God be thanked. *(Cut Exeter's line 117, "Tis wonderful!" or incorporate it into Henry to keep the scansion.)*

HENRY V   *Henry V*   5:57

Act V, sc. ii, lines 124-132, 136-175, 180-186, 188-199, 209-222, 226-230, 235-266 (prose)

Henry V awkwardly, but charmingly bumbles through his courting of Katharine of France.

(To make smooth transitions between speeches, cut Henry's questions to Katharine; often this will mean cutting the entire last sentence of a speech. An exception would be, "How answer you, la plus belle Katharine due monde, mon très cher et devin déesse." Also delete questions at the beginning of speeches if necessary and sometimes opening phrases or clauses. This can be a great speech if carefully edited.)

HENRY VI   *Henry VI, Part III*   2:42

Act II, sc. v, lines 1-54 (verse, soliloquy)

King Henry wishes that he were a shepherd instead of a king: "This battle fares like to the morning's war."

HENRY VI   *Henry VI, Part III*   1:54

Act III, sc. i, lines 13-54 (verse, soliloquy)

King Henry reasons that Warwick rather than Queen Margaret will receive the French king's favor.

(Cut both Keeper's lines.)

HENRY VI   *Henry VI, Part III*   2:13

Act V, sc. vi, lines 7-60 (verse)

Mourning his son's murder, King Henry goads Gloucester into killing him: "Hadst thou been kill'd when first thou didst presume,/Thou hadst not lived to kill a son of mine."

(Cut all of Gloucester's speeches.)

HENRY VIII   *Henry VIII*   3:57

Act II, sc. iv, lines 134-143, 155-209, 217-230 (verse)

King Henry, miserable about the trial regarding his marriage to Katharine, explains to the court that his conscience drove him to call the trial: "My conscience first received a tenderness,/Scruple, and prick."

HENRY VIII	*Henry VIII*	**2:54**

Act V, sc. i, lines 91-157 (verse)

King Henry tells Cranmer that he must reside in the Tower until he is brought to trial and gives him his ring as a sign of trust: "If entreaties/Will render you no remedy, this ring/Deliver them, and your appeal to us/There make before them." A difficult monologue because of Henry's commands to Cranmer to give him his hand, to stand, etc.

HENRY VIII	*Henry VIII*	**2:10**

Act V, sc. iii, lines 122-147, 154-163, 175-182 (verse)

King Henry upbraids the council for humiliating Cranmer rather than treating him as an equal: "Was it discretion lords, to let this man,/This good man—few of you deserve that title—/This honest man, wait like a lousy footboy/At chamber door? and one as great as you are?"
(Cut Surrey's line.)

HOTSPUR	*Henry IV, Part I*	**2:03 X**

Act I, sc. iii, lines 29-69 (verse)

"My liege, I did deny no prisoners." Hotspur reveals his temper and code of honor. The "popinjay" speech.

HOTSPUR	*Henry IV, Part I*	**1:30**

Act I, sc. iii, lines 158-187 (verse)

Hotspur castigates his father and uncle regarding their parts in King Richard's deposition and King Henry's ascension to the throne. With his usual energy, Hotspur points out that they may redeem themselves.

HOTSPUR	*Henry IV, Part I*	**1:54**

Act II, sc. iii, lines 1-38 (verse)

Hotspur reads and comments on a letter from a lord who declines to join Hotspur's rebellion. An excellent character speech that reveals Hotspur's impatience and zeal.

HOTSPUR	*Henry IV, Part I*	**3:00**

Act IV, sc. iii, lines 52-111 (verse)

Hotspur cites his quarrel with Henry IV: "Disgraced me in my happy victories,/Sought to entrap me by intelligence..."
(Incorporate and change Blunt's line to read, "Tut, you came not to hear this.")

IACHIMO   *Cymbeline*   2:03
Act II, sc. ii, lines 11-51 (verse)
Iachimo views the sleeping Imogen, steals her bracelet, and describes a mole on her breast, so that he may pretend proof of having seduced her. A difficult speech requiring the ability to suggest the presence of Imogen.

IACHIMO   *Cymbeline*   2:39
Act V, sc. v, lines 140-208, 412-417 (verse)
Iachimo confesses how he faked the evidence of having seduced Imogen and offers his regrets.
(Cut Cymbeline's lines as well as Iachimo's "All too soon I shall,/Unless thou would'st grieve quickly" in lines 170-171.)

IAGO   *Othello*   2:43
Act I, sc. i, lines 8-65 (verse)
Iago recounts his ire at being passed over in promotion for Michael Cassio and explains that this is part of the reason why he hates Othello: "But I will wear my heart upon my sleeve/For daws to peck at."
(Begin with "Three great ones of the city...;" cut Roderigo's lines.)

IAGO   *Othello*   4:24
Act I, sc. iii, lines 312-380, 387-410 (prose monol/verse soliloquy)
Iago's advice to Roderigo: "Put money in thy purse," followed by his evaluation of Roderigo and his plans for Othello: "Hell and night/Must bring this monstrous birth to the world's light."
Cut Roderigo's lines and Iago's "Virtue, a fig" in line 322.

IAGO   *Othello*   4:21
Act II, sc. i, lines 215-253, 262-288, 295-321 (prose monologue/verse soliloquy)

Iago convinces Roderigo and himself that Desdemona loves Cassio and that Othello has slept with Emilia: "They met so near with their lips that their breaths embraced together."
(*Cut Roderigo's lines.*)

IAGO	*Othello*	1:21

Act II, sc. i, lines 295-321 (verse, soliloquy)
"Knavery's plain face is never seen till used."

IAGO	*Othello*	1:20

Act II, sc. iii, lines 342-368 (verse, soliloquy)
"And what's he then that says I play the villain?"

JACQUES	*As You Like It*	1:18 ✗

Act II, sc. vii, lines 141-166 (verse)
"All the world's a stage..."

JAQUES	*As You Like It*	2:27

Act II, sc. vii, lines 12-61 (verse)
Jaques: "A fool, a fool! I met a fool i' the forest, / A motley fool; a miserable world."
(*Change Duke Senior's line 44 to read, "I shall have one," and incorporate it into the speech. Cut Duke Senior's other lines.*)

JOHN	*King John*	2:06

Act III, sc. iii, lines 19-64 (verse)
King John hints broadly to Hubert that he wants Arthur dead.
(*Cut Hubert's lines and John's line 58.*)

JOHN	*King John*	2:42

Act IV, sc. ii, lines 203-269 (verse)
King John, believing Hubert has killed Arthur, regrets Hubert's obedience. Then he learns that Arthur is alive and is relieved.
(*Cut Hubert's lines.*)

LAUNCE	*Two Gentlemen*	1:45

Act II, sc. iii, lines 1-35 (prose, soliloquy)

Launce describes his farewell to his family: "Nay, 'twill be
this hour ere I have done weeping."
(Speaks to his dog.)

| **LAUNCE** | *Two Gentlemen* | **2:12** |

Act IV, sc. iv, lines 1-44 (prose, soliloquy)
   Launce scolds his dog for committing an indiscretion:
"When did'st thou see me heave up my leg and make water
against a gentlewoman's farthingale?"
(Must indicate the dog.)

| **LAUNCELOT** | *Merchant of Venice* | **1:39 ✗** |

Act II, sc. ii, lines 1-33 (verse, soliloquy)
   Launcelot argues with his conscience and the devil about
running away from his master, Shylock. The devil wins.

| **LEAR** | *King Lear* | **1:07** |

Act II, sc. iv, lines 267-289 (verse)
   Lear curses his daughters: "No, you unnatural hags,/I
will have such revenges on you both,/That all the world
shall–I will do such things–/What they are, yet I know not;
but they shall be/The terrors of earth."

| **LEAR** | *King Lear* | **1:36** |

Act III, sc. ii, lines 1-9, 14-24, 49-60 (verse)
   Three speeches by Lear on the heath in the storm: "Blow
winds and crack your cheeks. . ."

| **LEAR** | *King Lear* | **4:24** |

Act IV, sc. iv, lines 83-191 (verse)
   Lear, mad, raves and rages about sin and lechery: "Die for
adultery! No:/The wren goes to't and the small gilded
fly/Does lecher in my sight."
(Cut Edgar's and Gloucester's lines.)

| **LEAR** | *King Lear* | **1:09 ✗** |

Act V, sc. iii, lines 257-63, 265-67, 269-74, 305-311 (verse)
   Lear dies over Cordelia's body: "Howl, howl, howl,
howl..."

LEONATO	*Much Ado*	**1:12**

Act IV, sc. i, lines 122-145 (verse)

Over-reacting to a charge of unchastity levelled at his daughter, Leonato decries the shame his daughter has thrust upon him.

LEONATO	*Much Ado*	**1:51**

Act V, sc. i, lines 3-38, 42-44 (verse)

Leonato will not be comforted over the shame and death of this daughter, Hero.
(Cut Antonio's line 33.)

LEWIS	*King John*	**1:57**

Act V, sc. ii, lines 78-116 (verse)

Lewis tells the Papal Legate, Pandulph, that he went to war with England with the Church's blessing but, now that England has regained the Church's blessing, France will not back away from her rightful claims in England.
(Cut Pandulph's line.)

LORD	*As You Like It*	**1:57**

Act II, sc. i, lines 25-63 (verse)

The First Lord reports Jaques' reaction upon seeing a wounded stag. This monologue sets up our expectations of Jaques.
(Incorporate Duke Senior's line and a half into the speech.)

LORENZO	*Merchant of Venice*	**1:45**

Act V, sc. i, lines 54-88 (verse)

Lorenzo rhapsodizes on the moonlight and the music, which can tame wild beasts: "How sweet the moonlight sleeps upon this bank."
(Cut Jessica's line 69 and Lorenzo's following half line, or change the pronouns and incorporate it into Lorenzo's part.)

MACBETH	*Macbeth*	**1:24 ✗**

Act I, sc. vii, lines 1-28 (verse, soliloquy)

Macbeth's fears and doubts about killing Duncan: "If it were done when 'tis done..."

MACBETH	*Macbeth*	1:42 ✗

Act II, sc. i, lines 31-64 (verse, soliloquy)
Macbeth: "Is this a dagger which I see before me?"

MACBETH	*Macbeth*	1:15

Act III, sc. i, lines 48-72 (verse, soliloquy)
Macbeth contemplates the murder of Banquo: "To be thus is nothing;/But to be safely thus."

MACBETH	*Macbeth*	1:30 ✗

Act V, sc. v, lines 1-7, 9 15, 17-28, 49-52 (verse)
Selections from the scene in which Macbeth learns of Lady Macbeth's death: "Tomorrow, and tomorrow, and tomorrow." Requires the imaginary presence of Seyton and an understanding on the audience's part that Seyton has announced the queen's death.

MALVOLIO	*Twelfth Night*	5:48 ✗

Act II, sc. v, lines 26-195 (prose)
Malvolio's letter scene. He has been led to believe that Olivia loves him and discovers a forged love letter, purportedly from her, and reads it.
(Cut all lines except Malvolio's.)

MARCUS	*Titus Andronicus*	2:21

Act II, sc. iv, lines 11-57 (verse)
Marcus encounters Lavinia, his niece, who has just been raped and had her tongue cut out and her hands cut off.

MARULLUS	*Julius Caesar*	1:12

Act I, sc. i, lines 37-60 (verse)
Marullus berates a crowd of commoners who line the streets to welcome Caesar, who has defeated Pompey. Marullus is upset because this same crowd gave such a welcome to Pompey when he was in favor.

MELUN	*King John*	1:57

Act V, sc. iv, lines 10-48 (verse)

The dying Melun warns Salisbury and Pembroke that the French will kill them once France beats England: "Fly, noble English, you are bought and sold."
(Cut Salisbury's line.)

MENENIUS	*Coriolanus*	3:39

Act I, sc. i, lines 56-118, 131-167 (verse)

Menenius tells the parable of the stomach and the limbs.
(Cut the Citizen's lines, but include "why the great" from line 160 as part of the speech.)

MENENIUS	*Coriolanus*	2:33

Act II, sc. i, lines 51-106 (prose)

Menenius abuses the two tribunes of plebes as political hacks.
(Cut Brutus' speeches.)

MERCUTIO	*Romeo & Juliet*	2:30 ✗

Act I, sc. iv, lines 54-103 (verse)

Mercutio's Queen Mab speech: "O then, I see Queen Mab hath been with you."
(Cut Romeo's lines.)

MESSENGER	*Henry VI, Part I*	1:54

Act I, sc. i, lines 103-140 (verse)

A narrative Messenger speech.
(Cut Winchester's speech and cut "O, no!" in line 108.)

MESSENGER	*Henry VI, Part III*	1:03

Act II, sc. i, lines 45-47, 50-67 (verse)

The Messenger recounts the news of York's death.

MORE	*Sir Thomas More*	4:03

Lines 75-83, 87-102, 106-156, 161-165 (verse)

More quiets a mob who protest the rising cost of food that has resulted from an influx of foreigners: "Look, what you do offend you cry upon."

MOROCCO	*Merchant of Venice*	3:06

Act II, sc. vii, lines 13-77 (verse)

The Prince of Morocco ponders over and chooses the golden casket so that he may win Portia as his bride. He makes the wrong choice and leaves in disappointment. Blank verse changes to rhyming trochaic tetrameter.

(Cut Portia's lines.)

NORFOLK	*Henry VIII*	1:54

Act I, sc. i, lines 8-45 (verse)

Norfolk describes the splendor of the meeting between Henry VIII and Francis I at the Field of the Cloth of Gold: "Men might say/Till this time pomp was single, but not married/To one above itself."

(Cut Buckingham's lines and also cut "Then you lost/The view of earthly glory" in lines 13-14.)

OBERON	*Midsummer*	2:00

Act II, sc. i, lines 146-187 (verse)

Oberon sends Puck to pick a magic flower whose juice, when placed on the eyelids causes the person to love the next being it sees.

(Cut Puck's lines.)

OLD TALBOT	*Henry VI, Part I*	1:36

Act IV, sc. vii, lines 1-32 (verse)

Old Talbot's grief over his son's death: "Where is my other life? Mine own is gone." In rhymed couplets; the actor must suggest the son's body.)

OLIVER	*As You Like It*	2:21

Act IV, sc. iii, lines 99-121, 128-133, 140-157 (verse)

Oliver tells of his reconciliation with his brother, Orlando, who wrestled a lion to save him.

ORSINO	*Twelfth Night*	1:49 ✘

Act I, sc. i, lines 1-15, 19-23, 26-41 (verse)

The Duke, Orsino, loses himself in romance and rhapsodizes upon Olivia: "If music be the food of love, play on." *(Cut the second half of line 23. Include Valentine's lines 26-32 as part of Orsino.)*

OTHELLO	*Othello*	3:03

Act I, sc. iii, lines 76-94, 128-169 (verse)

Othello describes the "witchcraft" he used to win Desdemona's love: "She loved me for the dangers I had passed, / And I loved her that she did pity them."

OTHELLO	*Othello*	1:06 ✘

Act V, sc. 2, lines 1-22 (verse)

Othello speaks over the sleeping Desdemona, justifying to himself his resolve to kill her. "It is the cause, it is the cause, my soul."

PALAMON	*Two Noble Kinsmen*	3:24

Act V, sc. i, lines 70-137 (verse)

Palamon, about to fight to the death against his friend and kinsman, Arcite, prays to Venus to grant him success and the prize, Emilia.

PANDULPH	*King John*	2:12

Act III, sc. i, lines 253-297 (verse)

Pandulph threatens King Philip with excommunication if Philip doesn't do as the Church commands: "The better act of purposes mistook / Is to mistake again; though indirect, / Yet indirection thereby grows direct / And falsehood falsehood cures." A masterpiece of specious logic. *(Cut Philip's line.)*

PANDULPH	*King John*	3:15

Act III, sc. iv, lines 112-181 (verse)

Pandulph reasons with Lewis that Arthur's necessary death will mean King John's demise and Lewis' ascendancy to the English throne.

(Cut Lewis' lines except line 117, "All days...", which should be included as a question.)

PETRUCHIO	Taming of the Shrew	1:20

Act IV, sc.i, lines 191-214 (verse, soliloquy)
Petruchio explains his plan to tame Katharina: "Thus have I politicly begun my reign..."

PIRITHOUS	Two Noble Kinsmen	1:48

Act V, sc. iv, lines 48-84 (verse)
Pirithous describes the death of Arcite, how his horse reared and curshed him. Excellent descriptive verse.

POLONIUS	*Hamlet*	3:46 X

Act II, sc. ii, lines 86-128, 131-170 (prose/verse)
Polonius claims that Hamlet's mad with love for Ophelia: "That he is mad, 'tis true: 'tis true 'tis pity;/ And pity 'tis 'tis true."
(Cut Queen's and King's lines as well as "I would fain prove so" in line 131.)

PORTER	*Macbeth*	1:09 X

Act II, sc. iii, lines 1-23 (prose, soliloquy)
The Porter's speech.

PORTER'S MAN	*Henry VIII*	1:09

Act V, sc. iv, lines 40-62 (prose)
The Porter's Man describes some of the commoners who are carousing at the christening: "There is a fellow somewhat near the door, he should be a brazier by his face..."

POSTHUMUS	*Cymbeline*	1:45

Act II, sc. v, lines 1-35 (verse, soliloquy)
Posthumus, having been convinced his wife was false, rails against her, his mother, and all women: "Is there no way for men to be, but women/Must be half-workers?"

POSTHUMUS	*Cymbeline*	1:39

Act V, sc. i, lines 1-33 (verse)

Posthumus, believing Imogen dead by his order, regrets it and resolves to fight for the Britons against Rome.

POSTHUMUS	*Cymbeline*	**2:24**

Act V, sc. iii, lines 3-51 (verse)

Posthumus, in a "messenger speech," describes the battle, the flight of the cowards, and the courageous stand of Belarius and his boys.

(The Lord's line 13 must be cut or rewritten for Posthumus; e.g.: "There, in a lane...")

POSTHUMUS	*Cymbeline*	**1:21**

Act V, sc. iv, lines 3-29 (verse, soliloquy)

Posthumus welcomes his imprisonment and prays for death as atonement for killing Imogen.

PRINCE HAL	*Henry IV, Part I*	**1:09**

Act I, sc. ii, lines 218-240 (verse, soliloquy)

Prince Hal explains his wanton behavior as heir apparent of England: "I know you all." A difficult speech because both the wayward prince and the future Henry V must be seen.

PRINCE HAL	*Henry IV, Part I*	**1:42**

Act II, sc. iv, lines 4-37 (prose)

Prince Hal tells Poins about his plan to play a trick upon Francis, a drawer at the Boar's Head tavern.

PRINCE HAL	*Henry IV, Part I*	**1:33**

Act III, sc. ii, lines 129-159 (verse)

Prince Hal, stung by his father's criticism, swears to redeem himself by defeating the rebellious Hotspur: "Do not think so, you shall not find it so."

PRINCE HAL	*Henry IV, Part II*	**1:24**

Act IV, sc. v, lines 20-47 (verse, soliloquy)

Prince Hal, thinking his father has died in his sleep, puts on the crown laid near his father. Hal pledges to be a king his father would be proud of.

| **PRINCE HAL** | *Henry IV, Part II* | 1:57 |

Act IV, sc. v, lines 139-177 (verse)

Prince Hal pledges his fealty to his dying father and tries to comfort him by his promise of reform in his lifestyle.

| **PRINCE HAL** | *Henry IV, Part II* | 2:12 |

Act V, sc. ii, lines 102-145 (verse)

Prince Hal renounces his frivolous past and assumes the dignity of his rank; the new King Henry V assures the Lord Chief Justice of London that the past is forgiven and that he wishes the Chief Justice to continue in his office.

| **PRINCE HAL** | *Henry IV, Part II* | 1:18 |

Act V, sc. v, lines 51-76 (verse)

Prince Hal completes his transformation to King Henry V when he tells Falstaff, "I know thee not, old man..."

Note: "Prince Hal" becomes Henry V on his father's death; his speeches in the play Henry V can be found under the character name of "Henry V," on pages 39-41.

| **PROLOGUE** | *Henry VIII* | 1:36 |

Prologue, lines 1-32 (verse, soliloquy)

"I come no more to make you laugh."

(Rhymed couplets.)

| **PROSPERO** | *The Tempest* | 2:04 ✗ |

Act V, sc. i, lines 1-57 (verse)

Prospero intends to release his enemies from their enchantment: "But this rough magic/I here abjure."

(Cut Ariel's lines. Cut Prospero's line 3, "How's the day", lines 5-6, "I did...the tempest" and lines 118-20, "Dost thou...mine shall.")

| **PROSPERO** | *The Tempest* | 0:48 ✗ |

Epilogue, lines 1-20 (verse, soliloquy)

Prospero's farewell to his art: "Now my charms are all o'erthrown."

(20 lines of rhyming iambic tetrameter.)

PROTEUS	*Two Gentlemen*	2:09

Act II, sc. vi, lines 1-43 (verse, soliloquy)

   Proteus tries to resolve his fickle disdain for Julia and for Valentine and his fickle love for Silvia.

PUCK	*Midsummer*	1:26

Act V, sc. i, lines 378-397, 430-445 (verse)

   Puck describes night as the fairy's day and begs a farewell of the audience.

(Rhyming trochaic tetrameter.)

RICHARD II	*Richard II*	2:30

Act III, sc. ii, lines 4-26, 36-62 (verse)

   Richard weeps at being in England again and conjures the land to kill his enemies who dare challenge God's anointed.

RICHARD II	*Richard II*	2:48 ✘

Act III, sc. ii, lines 144-218 (verse)

   King Richard alternately despairs and hopes about retaining the crown: "Let's talk of graves, of worms and epitaphs/ Make dust our paper and with rainy eyes/Write sorrow on the bosom of the earth."

(Cut Aumerle's and Scroop's lines.)

RICHARD II	*Richard II*	2:24

Act III, sc. iii, lines 72-100, 121-130, 133-141 (verse)

   King Richard scolds Northumberland for his lack of protocol, gives in to Bolingbrooke's demands, and then regrets that he, the king, has debased himself so.

RICHARD II	*Richard II*	2:51

Act III, sc. iii, lines 143-209 (verse)

   King Richard decides to abdicate: "What must the King do now? Must he submit?"

(Cut Northumberland's and Bolingbrooke's lines except Bolingbrooke's line 209, "Yea, my good lord;" incorporate it into the speech.)

RICHARD II *Richard II* 5:15

Act III, sc. iii, lines 72-209 (verse)

At Flint Castle, King Richard agrees to abdicate: "Down, down I come, like glistering Phaeton,/Wanting the manage of unruly jades." A longer version of the above monologue. *(Extract all of Richard's speeches and incorporate Bolingbrooke's line 209, "Yea, my good lord.")*

RICHARD II *Richard II* 1:45

Act IV, sc. i, lines 162-199 (verse)

King Richard abdicates: "Alack, why am I sent for to a king/Before I have shook off the regal thoughts/Wherewith I reigned?"

(Cut Bolingbrooke's and York's lines except line 190, which change to read, "You thought I had been willing . . ." and incorporate it into the speech.)

RICHARD II *Richard II* 1:06

Act IV, sc. i, lines 201-222 (verse)

Asked if he is "contented to resign the crown," King Richard musters all his sense of the dramatic to deliver his abdication speech.

RICHARD II *Richard II* 5:54

Act IV, sc. i, lines 162-176, 181-193, 195-221, 229-242, 244-252, 255-267, 276-302 (verse)

King Richard abdicates; the deposition scene: "I have no name, not title,/No, not that name was given me at the font,/But 'tis usurped." A combination of the two preceding monologues, and a further continuation.

(Incorporate and rewrite thus: line 190 "You thought I had been willing to resign"; line 200 "Am I contented to resign the crown?"; line 292 "The shadow of my sorrow hath destroyed/The shadow of my face". Begin line 229 with "Gentle Northumberland..." and begin line 255 with "I have no name, no title." Finally, end this scene with "How to lament the cause.")

RICHARD II *Richard II* 3:16

Act V, sc.v, lines 1-66 (verse, soliloquy)

King Richard philosophizes about his deposition and imprisonment: "I have been studying how I may compare/ This prison where I live unto the world."

Note: King Richard III is still the Duke of Gloucester in Acts I-III; his character name in most texts is "Gloucester" in the speeches from these acts, although we use RICHARD III in the headings for the sake of clarity. For this character's speeches in Henry VI, Part III, see "Gloucester," page 35.

RICHARD III   *Richard III*   2:03 **✗**

Act I, sc. i, lines 1-41 (verse, soliloquy)

Richard, Duke of Gloucester plans to seize the throne: "Now is the winter of our discontent."

RICHARD III   *Richard III*   1:39

Act I, sc. ii, lines 152-184 (verse)

Richard, Duke of Gloucester swears he killed for love of Lady Anne: "But 'twas thy beauty that provoked me."

RICHARD III   *Richard III*   1:51 **✗**

Act I, sc. ii, lines 228-264 (verse)

Richard, Duke of Gloucester, having successfully wooed Lady Anne after killing her husband, asks: "Was ever woman in this humour woo'd?"

RICHARD III   *Richard III*   1:18

Act I, sc. iii, lines 324-41, 345-49, 354-56 (verse, monol/soliloquy)

Richard, Duke of Gloucester's soliloquy:"I do the wrong, and first begin to brawl." Then his instructions to the murderers: "Your eyes drop millstones, when fools' eyes drop tears."

(Cut the Murderers' lines and Richard's line 344, "Well thought upon...")

RICHARD III   *Richard III*   1:09

Act III, sc. v, lines 72-94 (verse)

Richard, Duke of Gloucester instructs Buckingham to "Infer the bastardy of Edward's children," and of Edward himself.

RICHARD III	*Richard III*	2:33

Act III, sc. vii, lines 141-173, 204-207, 223-236 (verse)

Gloucester (later Richard III) cleverly refuses, then accepts, Buckingham's offer of the crown: "Would you enforce me to a world of care?"

RICHARD III	*Richard III*	2:18

Act IV, sc. iv, lines 291-335 (verse)

King Richard glibly explains how his marrying Queen Elizabeth's daughter will right all the wrongs he has done to her: "Look, what is done cannot now be amended."

RICHARD III	*Richard III*	1:03

Act IV, sc. iv, lines 397-417 (verse)

King Richard argues that there can be no happiness for anyone unless Queen Elizabeth's daughter marries him: "As I intend to prosper and repent..."

RICHARD III	*Richard III*	1:30 ✗

Act V, sc. iii, lines 177-206 (verse, soliloquy)

King Richard's despair before the Battle of Bosworth Field: "There is no creature loves me."

RICHARD III	*Richard III*	1:54

Act V, sc. iii, lines 304-341 (verse)

King Richard's oration to his army: "Conscience is but a word that cowards use."

RICHMOND	*Richard III*	1:45

Act V, sc. iii, lines 236-270 (verse)

Richmond's oration to his troops: "More than I have said, loving countrymen,/The leisure and enforcement of the time/Forbids to dwell upon."

ROMEO	*Romeo & Juliet*	2:21

Act V, sc. iii, lines 74-120 (verse, soliloquy)

Romeo, having killed Paris in the Capulet tomb, lays his body next to Juliet. Thinking Juliet dead, Romeo drinks

poison and dies. The actor must be able to suggest the presence of the bodies of Paris, Juliet, and Tybalt.
(Begin with "Let me peruse this face.")

RUMOUR	*Henry IV, Part II*	2:00

Induction, lines 1-40 (verse, soliloquy)

Rumour provides the history necessary for the audience to understand *Henry IV, Part II.*

SHALLOW	*Henry IV, Part II*	2:18

Act III, sc. ii, lines 1-58 (prose)

Justice Shallow, an old man, reminiscing about his youth: "You had not four such swinge-bucklers in all the Inns o' Court again...and we knew where the bona-robas were..."
(Cut all of Silence's lines.)

SHYLOCK	*Merchant of Venice*	2:51

Act I, sc. iii, lines 107-178 (verse)

Shylock complains that Antonio criticizes usury except when he needs money, and suggests, "Let the forfeit/Be nominated for an equal pound /Of your fair flesh, to be cut off and taken/In what part of your body pleaseth me."
(Cut Antonio's and Bassanio's lines.)

SHYLOCK	*Merchant of Venice*	1:33 **✗**

Act III, sc. i, lines 46-76 (prose)

Shylock explains that he will take his pound of flesh: "It will feed my revenge." He expresses his bitterness at Antonio's anti-Semitism: "Hath not a Jew eyes?"
(Change Salarino's lines 53-54 to "forfeit, I will take his flesh" and incorporate it into Shylock's part.)

SHYLOCK	*Merchant of Venice*	1:24

Act IV, sc. i, lines 35-62 (verse)

Shylock's clever, eloquent answer to the duke's question as to why Shylock would rather have a pound of flesh than 3,000 ducats.

SUFFOLK	*Henry VI, Part II*	2:33

Act III, sc. ii 309-402 (verse)

As he goes into exile , Suffolk curses the king and bemoans his separation from the queen.
(Cut Margaret's and Vaux's speeches.)

SUFFOLK	*Henry VI, Part II*	2:12

Act IV, sc. i, lines 50-64, 67, 104-114, 121-130, 132-138 (verse)
Defiant and relying on his rank, Suffolk argues for his life and then accepts his impending death with bravado.

TIMON	*Timon of Athens*	2:03

Act IV, sc. i, lines 1-41 (verse)
Timon, turned misanthrope, curses Athens and all humanity.

TIMON	*Timon of Athens*	2:21

Act IV, sc. iii, lines 1-47 (verse, soliloquy)
Timon, living as a hermit, curses the world, digs for roots, and finds gold: "O blessed, breeding sun, draw from the earth/Rotten humidity."

TIMON	*Timon of Athens*	1:27

Act IV, sc. iii, lines 134-166 (verse)
Timon gives gold to two whores and rails at them, urging them to "whore still" and spread disease through the world.

TIMON	*Timon of Athens*	2:30

Act V, sc. i, lines 171-226 (verse)
Timon relishes the thought of the impending sack of Athens and offers the Athenians a tree where they may hang themselves.
(Cut Flavius' and the Senators' lines.)

TITUS	*Titus Andronicus*	2:09

Act III, sc. ii, lines 1-45 (verse)
Titus in grief and rage after his and Lavinia's hands have been cut off.
(Cut Marcus' lines.)

TITUS	*Titus Andronicus*	2:00

Act V, sc. ii, lines 167-206 (verse)

Titus slits the throats of Demetrius and Chiron, who raped and mutilated Lavinia. The actor needs to be able to place Lavinia, Publius, Chiron, and Demetrius.

TOUCHSTONE	*As You Like It*	1:24

Act V, sc. i, lines 32-40, 44-49, 51-63 (prose)
Touchstone bullies William out of courting Audrey.

TOUCHSTONE	*As You Like It*	1:48

Act V, sc. iv, lines 69-108 (prose)
Touchstone explains the refinements of a quarrel at court: "The lie direct."
(Begin with and incorporate Jaques' line with the following change: "But, for the seventh cause; how did I find the quarrel on the seventh cause?" Cut the rest of Jaques' lines.)

TYRREL	*Richard III*	1:09

Act IV, sc. iii, lines 1-23 (verse, soliloquy)
Tyrrel recounts the murder of the young Duke of York and Prince Edward which King Richard hired him for: "The tyrannous and bloody deed is done."

ULYSSES	*Troilus & Cressida*	3:06

Act i, sc. iii, lines 75-137 (verse)
Ulysses explains that Troy still stands because the Greeks are undisciplined. The "degree" speech: "The specialty of rule hath been neglected."

ULYSSES	*Troilus & Cressida*	6:33

Act I, sc. iii, lines 75-212 (verse)
Ulysses explains that Troy still stands because the Greeks are undisciplined. He cites Achilles' sulking and Thersites' mockeries.
(Include Nestor's speeches as part of Ulysses' part, but cut lines 138-141 and lines 186-187.)

ULYSSES	*Troilus & Cressida*	2:17

Act III, sc. iii, lines 145-190 (verse)
Ulysses on fame and oblivion: "Time hath, my lord, a wallet on his back."

WARWICK	*Henry IV, Part II*	**1:36**

Act III, sc. ii, lines 149, 153-157, 160-178, 188-194 (verse)

Over Gloucester's corpse, Warwick accuses Suffolk of the duke's murder.

WARWICK	*Henry VI, Part III*	**1:54**

Act II, sc. i, lines 104-141 (verse)

Warwick recounts how he fled the queen's army because his own army lost the will to fight. A narrative speech.

WARWICK	*Henry VI, Part III*	**1:12**

Act V, sc. ii, lines 5-28 (verse, soliloquy)

Warwick's death soliloquy: "Why, what is pomp, rule, reign, but earth and dust?"

WOLSEY	*Henry VIII*	**1:06**

Act II, sc. iv, lines 84-105 (verse)

Wolsey pleads his innocence of Queen Katharine's charge that he is her enemy: "I do profess/You speak not like yourself."

WOLSEY	*Henry VIII*	**0:51**

Act III, sc. ii, lines 85-104 (verse)

Wolsey privately rages over King Henry's secret marriage to Anne Bullen because he had arranged for Henry to marry the French king's sister" "To be her mistress' mistress! the Queen's queen!"

(Cut Norfolk's and Suffolk's speeches.)

WOLSEY	*Henry VIII*	**1:15**

Act III, sc. ii, lines 203-227 (verse soliloquy)

Wolsey upbraids himself for "negligence": "What should this mean?"

WOLSEY	*Henry VIII*	**1:09**

Act III, sc. ii, lines 350-372 (verse, soliloquy)

Wolsey's farewell. He realizes his power is gone and he has fallen: "And when he falls, he falls like Lucifer,/Never to hope again."

WOLSEY	*Henry VIII*	3:06

Act III, sc. ii, lines 373-376, 378-390, 407-459 (verse)

After his fall from power, Wolsey advises Cromwell to serve God and King before himself: "Love thyself last. Cherish those hearts that hate thee;/Corruption wins not more than honesty."
(Cut line 387, "I hope I have;" line 407, "There was the...me down" and line 458, "So I have." Cut all of Cromwell's lines.)

YORK	*Henry VI, Part II*	2:18

Act I, sc. i, lines 214, 259 (verse, soliloquy)

York reveals his dashed hopes and his firm resolve to fight the House of Lancaster to gain the crown he claims.

YORK	*Henry VI, Part II*	2:39

Act III, sc. i, lines 331-383 (verse, soliloquy)

York reveals his plans to gain the crown: "Now, York, or never, steel thy fearful thoughts."

YORK	*Henry VI, Part III*	1:18

Act I, sc. iv, lines 1-26 (verse)

York, weak from battle, resolves to stand and die: "The army of the Queen hath got the field."

YORK	*Henry VI, Part III*	2:48

Act I, sc. iv, lines 111-168 (verse)

York accuses Queen Margaret of denying her femininity because she gloats over his son's death and his misfortunes: "O tiger's heart wrapt in a woman's hide."
(Cut Northumberland's lines.)

YORK	*Richard II*	2:36

Act II, sc. i, lines 163-214 (verse)

York pleads with King Richard not to seize John of Gaunt's lands and revenues: "How long shall I be patient? Ah, how long/Shall tender duty make me suffer wrong?"

YORK	*Richard II*	2:00

Act II, sc. ii, lines 78-85, 88-91, 98-122 (verse)

   As Lord Governor of England, the harried York must deal with Bolingbrooke's invasion of England: "Comfort's in Heaven, and we are on the earth,/Where nothing lives but crosses, cares, and grief."

YORK	*Richard II*	1:54

Act V, sc. ii, lines 8-45 (verse)

   Sadly, York describes Bolingbrooke's procession into London with the deposed King Richard.

(Cut the Duchess' line 22 and give her line 41 to York.)

SCENES FOR TWO MEN

Listed in alphabetical order by play title, then in Act/scene order.

ALL'S WELL   *Parolles/Lafeu*   **4:39**

Act II, sc. iii, lines 191-283 (prose)

Lafeu insults Parolles who is too much a coward to challenge him.

ANTONY & CLEO.   *Antony/Enobarbus*   **3:57**

Act I, sc. ii, lines 126-204 (prose)

Antony, hearing of his wife Fulvia's death, resolves to break off from Cleopatra. Enobarbus ironically dispraises both Cleopatra and Fulvia.

ANTONY & CLEO.   *Enobarbus/Menas*   **3:03**

Act II, sc. vi, lines 85-145 (prose)

Enobarus and Menas, the land-thief and water-thief, greet each other with wary respect.

(Begin with "You and I have known, sir.")

AS YOU LIKE IT   *Oliver/Charles*   **4:03**

Act I, sc. i, lines 100-180 (prose)

Charles, a wrestler to the usurping duke, Frederick, fills Oliver in on the usurpation and asks permission from Oliver to fight fairly without fear of reprisal. Oliver assures him, "I had as lief thou didst break his neck as his finger." A lot of exposition for actors to deal with.

AS YOU LIKE IT   *Jaques/Amiens* ·   **3:15**

Act II, sc. v, lines 1-65 (prose)

Amiens and Jaques sing "Under the Greenwood Tree." They banter about songs, melancholy, and the duke.

(Amiens must sing well; Jaques should be able to carry a tune.)

AS YOU LIKE IT   *Touchstone/Corin*   **4:00**

Act III, sc. ii, lines 11-90 (prose)

Touchstone teases Corin with the thought that Corin is damned because he has never been to court. Corin almost outwits Touchstone with his reply that "good manners at court are as ridiculous in the country as the behaviour of the country is most mockable at the court."

AS YOU LIKE IT   *Jaques/Orlando*   2:12

Act III, sc. ii, lines 269-312 (prose)

Jaques and Orlando banter wittily about their dislike for each other: "I do desire we may be better strangers."

COMEDY OF ERRORS   *Antipholus/Dromio of S.*   5:30

Act II, sc. ii, lines 1-110 (prose)

Antipholus of Syracuse beats Dromio of Syracuse and quarrels with him. Low comedy, low puns.

COMEDY OF ERRORS   *Antipholus/Dromio of S.*   4:57

Act III, sc. ii, lines 71-169 (prose)

Dromio of Syracuse describes the fatness of Nell to Antipholus of Syracuse. The scene features an extended conceit of Nell as a globe of the world: "In what part of her body stands Ireand?" "Marry, sir, in her buttocks: I found it out by the bogs." Antipholus is a straight man.

CORIOLANUS   *Menenius/First Citizen*   6:09

Act I, sc. i, lines 15-25, 56-167 (verse/prose)

Menenius and the First Citizen: Menenius tells the parable of the stomach and the limbs.

(The Citizen is mostly prose and has only 35% of the lines.)

CORIOLANUS   *Cominius/Coriolanus*   4:35

Act I, sc. ix, lines 1-94 (verse)

After the victory at Corioli, Cominius praises Marcius and gives him his surname, Coriolanus. Coriolanus resists, but accepts the honors.

(Cut Lartius' first two speeches; give his third to Cominius as well as the line tagged, "All.")

CORIOLANUS   *Brutus/Sicinius*   3:18

Act II, sc. i, lines 221-286 (verse)

Sicinius and Brutus, tribunes of the plebes, who think Coriolanus is overproud, plot to disgrace him.

(Incorporate the Messenger's speech into Sicinius' part by changing the opening "You are" to "I am.")

CORIOLANUS	*Brutus/Sicinius*	4:08

Act II, sc. iii, lines 184-270 (verse)

Sicinius and Brutus, tribunes of the plebes, upbraid the people for acquiescing in the election of Coriolanus to the consulship, and instruct them how to get the election revoked.

(Cut the Citizens' lines and the line tagged "All.")

CORIOLANUS	*Brutus/Sicinius*	7:26

Act II, sc. i, lines 221-286 and Act II, sc. iii, lines 184-270 (verse)
(For a longer scene, combine the two selections above.)

CORIOLANUS	*Adrian/Nicanor*	2:85

Act IV, sc. iii, lines 1-57 (prose)

A Roman, Nicanor, and a Volsce, Adrian, meet and discuss Coriolanus' banishment.

CORIOLANUS	*Coriolanus/Aufidius*	4:48

Act IV, sc. v, lines 58-153 (verse)

Coriolanus, banished from Rome, goes to his old enemy, Aufidius, the Volsce, and offers to betray Rome.

CORIOLANUS	*Cominius/Menenius*	2:27

Act IV, sc. vi, lines 80-128 (verse)

Menenius says, "I told you so," when Cominius brings the news that Coriolanus and Aufidius are marching on Rome.

(Incorporate Brutus' line and the line tagged Both Tribunes, into Menenius' part.)

CYMBELINE	*Iachimo/Posthumus*	5:52

Act I, sc. iv, lines 60-182 (prose)

Iachimo wagers that he can seduce Posthumus' wife, Imogen.

(Iachimo begins with the Frenchman's line 60, "It was much like the argument..." and continues with his own speech. Cut Philario's lines and Iachimo's line 60, "By the gods, it is one.")

CYMBELINE   *Cloton/Lord*   **3:30**

Act II, sc. i, lines 1-70 (prose/verse)

Cloten pouts because no one will fight with him because he is the queen's son. The Lords humor him while making jokes at his expense.

(Combine the two Lords into one role.)

CYMBELINE   *Iachimo/Posthumus*   **5:51**

Act II, sc. iv, lines 26-149 (verse)

Iachimo fraudulently wins his bet with Posthumus, claiming he has seduced Imogen. He describes her bedroom and a mole on her breast, and shows Posthumus her bracelet.

(Incorporate Philario's first two speeches into Posthumus' part. Cut the rest of Philario's lines as well as Iachimo's lines 38-39.)

HAMLET   *Hamlet/Horatio*   **4:51**

Act I, sc. ii, lines 160-259 (prose/verse)

Horatio tells Hamlet about seeing his father's ghost.

(Cut: "Marcellus" in line 165, "Good even, sir" in line 167, "Longer, longer" in line 239, and "Not when I saw't" in line 240. Incorporate Marcellus' and Bernardo's lines into Horatio's part. Change pronouns where necessary.)

HAMLET   *Hamlet/Ghost*   **5:36**

Act I, sc. v, lines 1-112 (verse)

Hamlet meets his father's Ghost who describes his murder and swears Hamlet to revenge: "Murder most foul, as in the best it is;/But this most foul, strange and unnatural."

(The Ghost has 2/3 of the lines.)

HAMLET   *Hamlet/Polonius*   **4:28**

Act II, sc. ii, lines 170-223, 405-439 (prose)

Polonius "boards" Hamlet to try his madness. Hamlet teases Polonius. Polonius tells Hamlet that the actors have arrived.

HAMLET	*Hamlet/Ros. & Guild.*	**4:09**

Act III, sc. ii, lines 307-389 (prose)

The recorder scene: Rosencrantz and Guildenstern fetch Hamlet to the queen after "The Murder of Gonzago."
(Collapse Rosencrantz and Guildenstern into one role; this will balance the parts.)

HAMLET	*Hamlet/Claudius*	**2:42**

Act IV, sc. iii, lines 17-70 (prose/verse)

Hamlet tells Claudius where Polonius' body is: "But indeed, if you find him not within this month, you shall nose him as you go up the stairs into the lobby."

HAMLET	*1st Clown/2nd Clown*	**3:36**

Act V, sc. i, lines 1-72 (prose)

The gravedigger scene: the 1st Clown and the 2nd Clown tell jokes and riddles about death, etc.
(The 1st Clown has 75% of the lines; the 2nd Clown has 25%.)

HAMLET	*Hamlet/1st Clown*	**4:27**

Act V, sc. i, lines 127-215 (prose)

The 1st Clown (the gravedigger) tells Hamlet about the events in the palace and also tells him about whose grave he is digging up. "Alas, poor Yorick! I knew him, Horatio; a fellow of infinite jest, of most excellent fancy."
(Cut references to Horatio.)

HAMLET	*Hamlet/Osric*	**5:31**

Act V, sc. ii, lines 81-190 (prose)

Osric invites Hamlet to duel with Laertes. The scene parodies Elizabethan courtly speech.

HENRY IV, Part I	*Prince Hal/Falstaff*	**5:51**

Act I, sc. ii, lines 1-117 (prose)

This scene is a first look at Sir John Falstaff and Henry, Prince of Wales. These two dissolutes trade good-natured insults and decide to stage a robbery the next day. Falstaff teases Hal about being heir apparent to the English throne, and Hal insults Falstaff about his girth.

HENRY IV, Part I   *Prince Hal/Poins*   3:06

Act I, sc. ii, lines 179-240 (prose/verse)

Poins persuades Prince Hal to join him in robbing Falstaff, Bardolph, Peto, and Gadshill, whom Poins has earlier persuaded to rob some pilgrims and traders. Ends with Hal's "I know you all" soliloquy.

HENRY IV, Part I   *Hotspur/Worcester*   8:47

Act I, sc. iii, lines 125-302 (verse)

Hotspur and his uncle, Worcester, are in rebellion against the king. Worcester tries to plan the strategy for the rebellion while Hotspur continually interrupts, raging against the king's injustices to him and to Mortimer; "I'll have a starling shall be taught to speak/Nothing but 'Mortimer' and give it him."

(Worcester takes all Northumberland's lines except his lines 130, 138, and 300 which are cut. Rewrite line 265 to read, "Being in Scotland thus employed, your father...")

HENRY IV, Part I   *Gadshill/Chamberlain*   2:45

Act II, sc. i, lines 52-106 (prose)

Gadshill and the Chamberlain of an inn banter back and forth. The Chamberlain gives Gadshill information about how much money certain guests at the inn carry so that Gadshill will know who to rob. A low comedy scene that takes a great deal of skill to do well.

(Chamberlain has 40% of the lines; Gadshill has 60%.)

HENRY IV, Part I   *Prince Hal/Falstaff*   9:09

Act II, sc. iv, lines 125-313 (prose)

Prince Hal baits Falstaff into boasting about the unsuccessful robbery at Gadshill. Falstaff tells of fighting off scores of men. Then Hal says in fact he and Poins alone drove off Falstaff and his men and robbed them.

(Hal has 36% of the lines; Falstaff has 64%. Cut Falstaff's lines 189-191, "Let them...darkness"), 197-198 "You rogue...Jew.", Peto's line 196, "No, no...", Poins' line 221 "Ay, ay...", and the

*first half of Hal's line 231 "Prithee...alone". The rest of Poins'
lines are taken by Hal; Gadshill's lines by Falstaff.)*

HENRY IV, Part I	*Prince Hal/Falstaff*	8:00

Act II, sc. iv, lines 358-528 (prose)

Prince Hal learns from Falstaff that Hotspur has raised an
army to depose King Henry. First Falstaff, then Hal pretend
to be the king, judging first Hal, then Falstaff. A comic scene
of one-up-manship, written in parody of the Euphistic prose
style of John Lyly.

*(Hal has 31% of the lines; Falstaff has 69%. Cut lines 430-441 "O
Jesu...good ticklebrain." Hal takes Poins' line 374.)*

HENRY IV, Part I	*Prince Hal/Falstaff*	18:39

*Act II, sc. iv, lines 125-313, 358-528 and Act I, sc. ii, lines 218-
240 (prose)*

Combine earlier cited scenes between Prince Hal and
Falstaff.

*(The soliloquy is added to improve the balance since the two scenes
are more that 60% Falstaff. The soliloquy, though earlier in the
play, plays best in this instance after the two scenes. Some narration should be inserted between the two scenes.)*

HENRY IV, Part I	*Prince Hal/Hotspur*	2:03

Act V, sc. iv, lines 59-101 (verse)

A scene for two fencers. Prince Hal kills Hotspur and
delivers a eulogy over his body.

*(Cut Falstaff's lines 75-76. Hotspur has 37% of the lines, but the
main point of the scene is the fencing.)*

HENRY IV, Part II	*Falstaff/Justice*	7:48

Act I, sc. ii, lines 105-260 (prose)

Falstaff is accosted by the Lord Chief Justice of London,
who tells Falstaff that his exploit at Gadshill is forgiven because of his service to England at Shrewsbury, but that he
wishes Falstaff would stay away from Prince Hal.

(The Justice has 37% of the lines; Falstaff has 63%.)

HENRY IV, Part II	*Prince Hal/Poins*	5:48

Act II, sc. ii, lines 1-73, 115-156 (prose)

Prince Hal and Poins rag each other over what being friends does for their credit in the world. Poins reads a letter from Falstaff informing Hal that Poins intends to get his sister, Nell, married to Hal.

(Add a line for Poins, something like, "But here is a letter to thee from Falstaff," to bridge the two parts of the scene.)

HENRY IV, Part II   *Henry/Warwick*   **3:51**

Act III, sc. i, lines 32-108 (verse)

King Henry, ill, talks to Warwick about the troubled realm: "O God! that one might read the book of fate." Warwick tells him the troubles were inevitable.

(Warwick has 39% of the lines; the King has 61%.)

HENRY IV, Part II   *Henry/Prince Hal*   **6:42**

Act IV, sc. iv, lines 92-225 (verse)

As King Henry dies, he and his son, Prince Hal, reconcile their differences with each other. Not a real dialogue: two long speeches by the King; one by Hal.

(Hal has 1/3 of the lines; the King has 2/3.)

HENRY IV, Part II   *Morton/Northumberland*   **7:45**

Act I, sc. i, lines 60-215 (verse)

The Earl of Northumberland's retainer, Morton, returns to Warkworth from Shrewsbury to tell the earl that his son, Hotspur, is dead. The earl mourns for his son and with Morton's support is determined to carry on the rebellion.

(Cut Lord Bardolph's line 104, but incorporate the rest of Lord Bardolph's as well as Travers' lines into Morton's part.)

HENRY V   *Henry/Montjoy*   **2:48**

Act III, sc. vi, lines 121-176 (verse/prose)

Montjoy, a French herald, brings word from the French king that Henry V will regret his invasion of France. Henry admits his men are sick, but warns that they will fight valiantly, though they want to rest awhile at Calais.

(86% of the scene is two speeches, one by each actor.)

HENRY V   *Henry/Michael Williams*   **7:24**

Act IV, sc. i, lines 91-238 (prose)

The night before the Battle of Agincourt, Henry V in disguise goes round to his troops to encourage them. Michael Williams and he argue about the relationship between a king and his soldiers. They exchange tokens by which they may identify each other so that they may continue the quarrel after the battle should they survive.
(Williams has 37% of the lines; Henry has 63%.)

HENRY VI, Part I   *Talbot/John*   7:09

Act IV, sc. v, lines 1-55; sc. vi, lines 1-57; and sc. vii, lines 1-32 (verse)

Talbot urges his son, John, to flee the battle; John refuses. John is slain; Talbot dies of grief. Almost entirely in rhymed couplets.
(John has 1/3 of the lines; Talbot has 2/3; cut the Servant's line.)

HENRY VI, Part II   *Cade/Lord Say*   5:12

Act IV, sc. vii, lines 26-132 (prose/verse)

Jack Cade, rebel leader, sentences Lord Say to death for losing France and for being literate.
(Cut Dick's lines 57-58 and line 120, tagged "All;" Cade takes the rest of the rebels' lines.)

HENRY VI, Part II   *Cade/Iden*   4:30

Act IV, sc. x, lines 1-90 (prose/verse)

Cade, who is starving, steals into the garden of Iden, who kills him for trespassing; Cade insists, "famine and no other hath slain me."
(Cade speaks prose; Iden speaks verse.)

HENRY VI, Part III   *Clifford/Rutland*   2:09

Act I, sc. iii, lines 10-52 (verse)

Clifford kills Rutland, the Duke of York's youngest son, in revenge for his father's death by York.

HENRY VI, Part III   *Henry/Gloucester*   4:38

Act V, sc. vi, lines 1-93 (verse)

Gloucester kills King Henry. Includes Gloucester's "What, will the aspiring blood of Lancaster/Sink in the ground?" soliloquy.

(Could use a Lieutenant briefly at beginning as a non-speaking role, but it's not essential.)

HENRY VIII	Norfolk/Buckingham	9:18

Act I, sc. i, lines 1-114, 120-197 (verse)

Norfolk recounts the splendid pomp of the meeting of Henry VIII and Francis I at the Field of Cloth of Gold. Unimpressed, Buckingham rages against Cardinal Wolsey's pride and extravagance.

(Cut Abergavenny's first speech and incorporate the rest of his lines into Buckingham's part.)

HENRY VIII	Two Gentlemen	4:24

Act II, sc. i, lines 1-54, 136-169 (verse)

Two Gentlemen discuss the current events: Buckingham's trial and execution and Queen Katharine's imminent demise via Cardinal Wolsey.

HENRY VIII	Henry/Wolsey	3:25

Act III, sc. ii, lines 135-203 (verse)

King Henry, having just learned of Wolsey's schemes and immense wealth, hints at his displeasure with Wolsey.
(Cut Surrey's lines.)

HENRY VIII	Porter/Porter's Man	3:24

Act V, sc. iv, lines 1-70 (prose)

The Porter and the Porter's Man describe the rabble that have crashed the christening of the infant Elizabeth.
(Cut the lines tagged "Within".)

JULIUS CAESAR	Cassius/Brutus	8:00

Act I, sc. ii, lines 25-188 (verse)

Cassius probes Brutus' feelings regarding the ascendancy of Julius Caesar, intending to involve him in the assassination conspiracy.
(Brutus has 1/3 of the lines; Cassius has 2/3.)

JULIUS CAESAR	Cassius/Brutus	11:18 X

Act IV, sc. ii, lines 37-52; Act IV, sc. iii, lines 1-123, 144-162, 196-230; and Act V, sc. i, lines 93-126 (verse)

Cassius and Brutus quarrel over the condemnation of Pella, a bribe-taker, and about Cassius' "itching palm." They are reconciled and Brutus tells of Portia's death. Cassius admires Brutus' stoicism. They plan the Battle of Philippi. There is a passage of time between Acts IV and V.

KING JOHN	*Arthur/Hubert*	**6:39**

Act IV, sc. i, lines 1-135 (verse)

Arthur persuades Hubert, his keeper, not to burn his eyes out.

(Cut the Executioner's lines 6 and 86 and indicate his presence.)

KING JOHN	*John/Hubert*	**4:25**

Act IV, sc. ii, lines 182-269 (verse)

Hubert tells King John of the talk of the upheaval in nature since Arthur's supposed death and John chastises Hubert for obeying his order to kill Arthur; Hubert confides to John that he hasn't killed Arthur.

KING JOHN	*Salisbury/Lewis*	**3:13**

Act V, sc. ii, lines 1-64 (verse)

Salisbury regrets that in order to be honorable he must fight for the French against England. Lewis, with great respect, consoles Salisbury.

(Basically two one-minute speeches of fine quality.)

KING JOHN	*Hubert/Philip*	**2:12**

Act V, sc. vi, lines 1-44 (verse)

Hubert urges the Philip the Bastard to hurry to King John's side because "The King, I fear, is poison'd by a monk."

KING LEAR	*Edmund/Gloucester*	**7:15**

Act I, sc. ii, lines 1-145 (prose/verse)

Using a forged letter Edmund persuades his father, Gloucester, that his brother Edgar intends to kill Gloucester.

KING LEAR	*Lear/Fool*	**2:21**

Act I, sc. v, lines 8-56 (prose)

Lear and the Fool: "O, let me not be mad."

(Cut the gentleman's line and Lear's line to him.)

KING LEAR	*Edmund/Gloucester*	**2:40**

Act II, sc. i, lines 35-87 (verse)

Edmund wounds himself in order to falsely persuade his father, Gloucester, that his brother Edgar meant to kill Gloucester. Gloucester outlaws Edgar and promises to raise Edmund in Edgar's stead.

KING LEAR	*Edgar/Gloucester*	**4:00**

Act IV, sc. vi, lines 1-80 (verse)

Edgar, disguised, leads Gloucester, blind, to Dover and makes him think he has survived a leap from the cliffs.

LOVE'S LABOURS	*Armado/Moth*	**6:27**

Act I, sc. ii, lines 1-129 (prose)

Armado and Moth discuss Armado's love (unrequited) for Jacquenetta. Puns, chop-logic, and fantastical conceits.

MACBETH	*Macduff/Malcolm*	**6:57**

Act IV, sc. iii, lines 1-139 (verse)

Macduff solicits Malcolm to return to Scotland as king. Malcolm declares his unworthiness: "Bleed, bleed, poor country!"

MACBETH	*Macbeth/Macduff*	**1:42**

Act V, sc. viii, lines 1-34 (verse)

Macduff kills Macbeth. A scene for two fencers; "Lay on Macduff."

(Macduff has 29% of the lines; Macbeth has 71%.)

MEASURE	*Duke/Lucio*	**5:31**

Act III, sc. ii, lines 91-200 (prose)

Lucio, thinking the Duke away and not recognizing him in his disguise as a friar, tells him about his (the Duke's) vices. The Duke tells Lucio he shall one day have to answer for his slanders. A mildly amusing scene.

MEASURE	*Duke/Provost*	7:33

Act IV, sc. ii, lines 75-226 (prose/verse)

Disguised as a friar, the Duke and the Provost devise a plan to save Claudio by executing a drunk, Barnardine, in Claudio's stead.

(Change: the 2nd half of line 103 to read, "That was his lordship's man"; line 104 to read, "And there is Claudio's pardon"; and the Messenger's speech to read, "My Lord hath sent me this note; and...this further charge, that I swerve not from the smallest article of it, neither in time, matter, or other circumstance." Incorporate this much of the speech into the Provost's part and cut the balance of it.)

MERCHANT	*Bassanio/Antonio*	3:39

Act I, sc. i, lines 113-185 (verse)

In love with Portia but short on money, Bassanio asks Antonio (all of whose money is in cargo at sea) for a loan so that he may court Portia.

MERCHANT	*Shylock/Antonio*	6:13

Act I, sc. iii, lines 60-182 (verse)

Shylock baits Antonio into agreeing to allow him to cut a pound of Antonio's flesh out of his body if he cannot repay his loan.

(Cut Bassanio's lines.)

MERCHANT	*Launcelot/Gobbo*	4:21

Act II, sc. ii, lines 34-120 (prose)

Launcelot befuddles his blind old father, Gobbo: giving him confusing directions to Shylock's house, telling him his son is dead, and generally giving him a hard time.

(Gobbo has 36% of the lines; Launcelot has 64%.)

MERCHANT	*Salanio/Salarino*	2:40

Act II, sc. viii, lines 1-53 (verse)

Salanio and Salarino make fun of Shylock's distress over losing both his daughter and jewels to Lorenzo. They also ponder over a rumor that Antonio's ship has sunk and the love Antonio shows toward Bassanio.

(Salanio has 40% of the lines; Salarino has 60%.)

MERRY WIVES	*Falstaff/Ford*	6:57

Act II, sc. ii, lines 160-298 (prose)

Ford, pretending to be Mr. Brook, engages Falstaff to seduce Mrs. Ford for him in order to discover if she is faithful.

(Falstaff has 40% of the lines; Ford has 60%.)

MERRY WIVES	*Falstaff/Ford*	4:55

Act III, sc. v, lines 58-155 (prose)

Falstaff tells Mr. Brook, the disguised Ford, about his attempt to seduce Mrs. Ford which led to him being thrown into a ditch from a laundry basket.

(Ford has 30% of the lines; Falstaff has 70%.)

MERRY WIVES	*Falstaff/Ford*	13:24

Act II, sc. ii, lines 160-329 and Act III, sc. v, lines 58-155 (prose)

A combination of the two Falstaff/Ford scenes already cited.

(To balance the parts better, Ford's soliloquy has been added to the first scene.)

MIDSUMMER	*Puck/Fairy*	2:47

Act II, sc. i, lines 1-59 (verse)

Puck and Fairy reveal the strife in the fairy kingdom and introduce themselves: "Over hill, over dale/Through bush, through brier."

(The entire scene is in rhyme.)

MIDSUMMER	*Puck/Oberon*	6:22

Act III, sc. ii, lines 1-42, 88-121, 345-400 (verse)

Puck has satisfactorily carried out Oberon's trick upon Titania but has failed Oberon's good intentions toward the four lovers. Oberon commands him to set things straight. The scene requires the imagined presence of the lovers.

(The scene is in rhymed couplets and includes 24 tetrameter lines.)

MUCH ADO	*Don John/Conrade*	3:45

Act I, sc. iii, lines 1-77 (prose)

Don John, a "plain dealing villain," learns from Conrade/ Borachio how he can spoil his brother Don Pedro's plans to marry Claudio and Hero.

(Conrade and Borachio are combined into one role. Cut Don John's line 42, "Who comes here?" and line 43, "What news, Conrade?" Change pronouns as needed.

OTHELLO   *Iago/Cassio*   5:30

Act II, sc. iii, lines 259-368 (prose/verse)

Cassio, having been dismissed by Othello, is counselled by Iago to sue to Desdemona to gain Othello's favor. "Reputation" scene.

OTHELLO   *Iago/Othello*   17:42

Act III, sc. iii, lines 35-40, 90-277, 321-480 (verse)

Iago makes Othello jealous, convincing him his wife is sleeping with Cassio.

(Othello remains onstage throughout; Iago reenters with a handkerchief. Cut the first half of line 330, "Look where he comes.")

OTHELLO   *Iago/Roderigo*   4:06

Act IV, sc. ii, lines 172-252 (prose)

Iago placates Roderigo, who threatens to go to Desdemona and ask her forgiveness; Iago suggests that Roderigo can still have Desdemona if they kill Cassio.

PERICLES   *Antiochus/Pericles*   7:21

Act I, sc. i, lines 1-149 (verse)

Antiochus offers his daughter's hand to the solver of a riddle, death to the suitor who fails to solve it. Pericles solves it and finds in it proof that the daughter and father are living in incest and, therefore, no longer wants her.

(Pericles has 2/3 of the lines. Cut the Daughter's lines. 1/3 of the scene is in rhyming couplets.)

RICHARD II   *Bolingbrooke/Gaunt*   2:51

Act I, sc. iii, lines 253-309 (verse)

Gaunt tries to console Bolingbrooke, his banished son, by minimizing the pains of exile. Bolingbrooke is unconvinced:

"O, who can hold a fire in his hand/By thinking on the frosty Caucasus"

RICHARD II   *Bolingbrooke/York*   **4:08**

Act II, sc. iii, lines 82-136, 140-147, 152-171 (verse)

York, Regent in England during Richard's absence, tries to dissuade Bolingbrooke from starting a civil war: "Grace me no grace, nor uncle me no uncle:/I am no traitor's uncle."

RICHARD II   *Richard/Scroop*   **3:15**

Act III, sc. ii, lines 76-142 (verse)

King Richard swings from depression to rage as Scroop tells him that England is in a state of civil war and that Bushy, Bagot, and Green are dead.

(Cut Aumerle's line 82 and give his line 141 to Richard.)

RICHARD III   *Richard/Buckingham*   **7:30**

Act III, sc. vii, lines 92-247 (verse)

Buckingham entreats the seemingly reluctant Duke of Gloucester to accept the crown. Gloucester refuses and then, finally, accepts—to become King Richard III.

(Cut lines 201-203, 221-222, and 241. Buckingham takes the Mayor's line 237.)

RICHARD III   *Richard/Buckingham*   **3:48**

Act IV, sc. ii, lines 1-31, 42-45, 86-126 (verse)

King Richard says to Buckingham about Prince Edward and his brother, "Shall I be plain I wish the bastards dead." Buckingham "grows circumspect" and reminds Richard of promises he has made to him. Richard ignores him and Buckingham flees "while my fearful head is on."

(Buckingham takes Catesby's line 27.)

ROMEO & JULIET   *Gregory/Sampson*   **2:30**

Act I, sc. i, lines 1-50 (prose)

The two Capulet servants, Sampson and Gregory, plan what action they'll take if they meet some of Montague's servants. A first look at the Capulet-Montague feud.

ROMEO & JULIET   *Romeo/Mercutio*   **5:42**

Act I, sc. iv, lines 1-114 (verse)

Mercutio encourages the melancholy Romeo to love again since Rosaline has rejected him. The two young men debate about love. The scene contains the "Queen Mab" speech.
(Mercutio takes Benvolio's lines. Romeo has 29% of the lines, Mercutio 71%—but Mercutio can easily be shortened for balance.

ROMEO & JULIET	Romeo/Fr. Laurence	3:12

Act II, sc. iii, lines 31-94 (verse)
Romeo asks Friar Laurence to marry him to Juliet, but Friar Laurence chides Romeo for his fickleness in love.
(Romeo has 1/3 of the lines; Friar Laurence has 2/3.)

ROMEO & JULIET	Romeo/Mercutio	3:29

Act II, sc. iv, lines 37-106 (prose)
Romeo and Mercutio compete in making dreadful puns: "O single-soled jest, solely singular for the singleness."

ROMEO & JULIET	Romeo/Fr. Laurence	4:00

Act III, sc. iii, lines 1-80 (verse)
Friar Laurence tries to comfort the frantic Romeo after he tells Romeo that he is banished from Verona.
(Requires the Nurse's voice from off-stage. Friar Laurence has 1/3 of the lines; Romeo has 2/3.)

TAMING of the SHREW	Lucentio/Tranio	3:45

Act I, sc. i, lines 151-225 (verse)
Lucentio and his servant, Tranio, trade clothes and social positions so that Lucentio may be near Bianca.

TEMPEST	Prospero/Ariel	5:54

Act I, sc. ii, lines 187-304 (verse)
Ariel tells Prospero how he staged the shipwreck and begs his freedom. Prospero calls him ungrateful and reminds him of his obligations to Prospero.

TEMPEST	Prospero/Caliban	2:48

Act I, sc. ii, lines 319-374 (verse)
Prospero tells Caliban why he is treated like a slave--for attempting to rape Miranda--and Caliban curses him.

(Lines 351-362 are listed as Miranda's lines in some editions, but, for this scene, are to be taken by Prospero.)

TEMPEST	*Antonio/Sebastian*	**4:54**

Act II, sc. i, lines 199-296 lines (verse)

Antonio convinces Sebastian to kill Alonso, his brother, so that Sebastian will become heir to the throne of Naples. Antonio reminds Sebastian that he became Duke of Milan by similar means and he's not had a twinge of conscience.

(Sebastian has 30% of the lines; Antonio has 70%.)

TIMON of ATHENS	*Timon/Flavius*	**5:24**

Act II, sc. ii, lines 133-242 (verse)

Flavius explains to Timon that Timon is bankrupt. Timon resolves to borrow from his friends.

(Cut Flaminius' and Servants' lines.)

TIMON of ATHENS	*Flaminius/Lucullus*	**3:03**

Act III, sc. i, lines 5-66 (prose/verse)

Flaminius, Timon's servant, goes to Lucullus to borrow money for his master. Lucullus gives him a bribe to say he never saw him.

(Cut the Servant's line.)

TIMON of ATHENS	*Sepromonius/Servant*	**2:06**

Act III, sc. iii, lines 1-42 (verse)

Timon's Servant goes to Sempronius to borrow money for his master. Sempronius pretends to be insulted and refuses: "The devil knew not what he did when he made man politic."

(Not much dialogue: 85% of the scene is two long speeches—one by each actor.)

TIMON of ATHENS	*Timon/Apemantus*	**11:09**

Act IV, sc. iii, lines 176-398 (prose/verse)

Timon and Apemantus curse each other and compete in misanthropy.

TIMON of ATHENS *Timon/Flavius* 4:03

Act IV, sc. iii, lines 463-543 (verse)

Flavius seeks out Timon in the woods to aid and comfort him, but is rejected.

TROILUS & CRESSIDA *Troilus/Pandarus* 4:33

Act I, sc. i, lines 1-91 (prose/verse)

Troilus and Pandarus discuss Troilus' love for Cressida. Troilus' lines are lyric verse; Pandarus' lines are colloquial prose. The scene is an opportunity for two actors with different skills.

TROILUS & CRESSIDA *Aeneas/Agamemnon* 4:09

Act I, sc. iii, lines 215-309 (verse)

Aeneas brings a challenge to Agamemnon and the Greeks. *(Cut Nestor's and Ullysses' lines. Agamemnon has 1/3 of the lines; Aeneas has 2/3.)*

TROILUS & CRESSIDA *Ulysses/Nestor* 4:10

Act I, sc. iii, lines 310-392 (verse)

Ulysses and Nestor plot to have Ajax accept a challenge from Hector as a means of ending Achilles' sulking.

TROILUS & CRESSIDA *Pandarus/Servant* 2:15

Act III, sc. i, lines 1-45 (prose)

Pandarus seeks information from Paris's Servant: "Friend, we understand not one another; I am too courtly, and thou art too cunning."

TROILUS & CRESSIDA *Ulysses/Achilles* 7:05

Act III, sc. iii, lines 74-215 (verse)

Ulysses and Achilles discuss fame and oblivion; why Achilles' reputation has slipped. *(Achilles has 25% of the lines; Ulysses has 75%.)*

TWELFTH NIGHT *Andrew/Toby* 3:21

Act I, sc. iii, lines 85-151 (prose)

Sir Toby teases and makes a fool of Sir Andrew, who seems unaware of it.

TWELFTH NIGHT   *Malvolio/Feste*   **6:09**

Act IV, sc. ii, lines 1-141 (prose)
Malvolio has been imprisoned in a dark room because his enemies have tricked him and convinced the countess he is mad. The Clown, Feste, comes to him as "Sir Topas," the curate, who is to restore his sanity and later, speaks as himself.

(The opening speeches can be edited thus: Feste: "I'll put on this gown and this beard; make him believe I am Sir Topas the curate." Then he reads his own speech, cutting the last sentence, and then going into "for as the old hermit..." in line 13. Then play the scene as written, cutting Toby's and Maria's lines.)

TWO GENTLEMEN   *Proteus/Valentine*   **3:27**

Act I, sc. i, lines 1-69 (verse)
Valentine and Proteus part. Valentine is setting sail for adventures in Milan, and Proteus is staying in Verona where his love, Julia, is.

TWO GENTLEMEN   *Proteus/Speed*   **4:36**

Act I, sc. i, lines 70-161 (prose)
Proteus asks Speed if he has delivered a love letter to Julia. Speed misconstrues and puns at all the questions.

TWO GENTLEMEN   *Valentine/Speed*   **4:54**

Act II, sc. i, lines 1-98 (prose)
Valentine plays straight man to his servant, Speed, as they discuss Silvia, Valentine's new love.

TWO GENTLEMEN   *Proteus/Valentine*   **4:39**

Act II, sc. iv, lines 122-214 (verse)
Proteus teases Valentine about Silvia and probes for information about her because he, too, loves her.

TWO GENTLEMEN   *Launce/Speed*   **3:06**

Act II, sc. v, lines 1-62 (prose)

Two clowns, Launce and Speed, discuss their masters'
mistresses.

TWO GENTLEMEN   *Duke/Valentine*   6:51

Act III, sc. i, lines 51-187 (verse)

Knowing that Valentine plans to elope with Silvia, the
Duke tricks him into revealing the elopement, and then
banishes him.

TWO GENTLEMEN   *Launce/Speed*   5:50

Act III, sc. i, lines 279-395 (prose)

A clown scene: Speed and Launce mull over a love letter
itemizing the virtues of Launce's love.

TWO NOBLE KINSMEN *Arcite/Palamon*   4:10

Act I, sc. ii, lines 1-83 (verse)

Arcite and Palamon, distressed with the corruption of
Thebes and its ruler, Creon, resolve to leave the city.

TWO NOBLE KINSMEN *Arcite/Palamon*   9:33

Act II, sc. i, lines 1-221 (verse)

Palamon and Arcite, in prison, profess their great
friendship for each other, saying they are in no prison because they are together. Then they see Emilia and quarrel
over who has the right to love her.
(Cut Emilia's and the Woman's lines.)

TWO NOBLE KINSMEN *Arcite/Palamon*   6:12

Act III, sc. i, lines 1-124 (verse)

Palamon and Arcite, now enemies because they both love
Emilia, meet in the woods. Palamon is in manacles. Arcite
promises to bring him food and a file for his chains so that
they may duel.

TWO NOBLE KINSMEN *Arcite/Palamon*   2:39

Act III, sc. iii, lines 1-53 (verse)

Arcite brings food and drink to Palamon, his former
friend, who is hiding in the woods, to strengthen him for
their planned duel. They get drunk, seem to resume
friendship, and quarrel again.

TWO NOBLE KINSMEN *Arcite/Palamon*   6:33

Act III, sc. vi, lines 1-131 (verse)

Palamon and Arcite, once friends, now enemies, meet in the woods to duel over Emelia. They arm each other, express their former friendship, and fight. The actors should be good fencers and the scene requires weapons and armor.

(The fight is, in the play, interrupted by Theseus, but the scene can end with the fight commencing.)

TWO NOBLE KINSMEN *Arcite/Palomon*   25:00

Act II, sc. i, lines 1-221; Act III, sc. i, lines 1-124; Act III, sc. iii, lines 1-53; and Act III, sc. vi, lines 1-131 (verse)

This combination of scenes show the transition from love to hate and a duel to the death between Arcite and Palamon.

(Narration is required to bridge the scenes.)

WINTER'S TALE   *Archidamus/Camillo*   2:30

Act I, sc. i, lines 1-50 (prose)

Archidamus of Bohemia and Camillo of Sicilia discuss the friendship of their kings and compliment each other's country.

(A characterless, prosy scene, but it is almost exactly balanced between the two roles.)

WINTER'S TALE   *Leontes/Camillo*   7:39

Act I, sc. ii, lines 212-364 (verse)

Camillo assures Leontes that his wife, Hermione, is not having an affair with Leontes' boyhood friend, Polixenes. Camillo hesitantly agrees to poison Polixenes if Leontes will restore Hermione to his favor.

WINTER'S TALE   *Polixenes/Camillo*   5:45

Act I, sc. ii, lines 351-465 (verse)

Puzzled over Leontes' sudden lack of hospitality, Polixenes persuades Camillo to tell him what has happened. Camillo confesses that he is to poison Polixenes. Polixenes plans to leave.

WINTER'S TALE	*Shepherd/Clown*	**4:15**

Act III, sc. iii, lines 59-143 (prose)

A Shepherd discovers the abandoned baby, Perdita. His son, the Clown, describes the death of Antigonus, killed by a bear, and the wreck of the ship that brought him. Not a comic scene, but rather grisly narration.

WINTER'S TALE	*Autolycus/Clown*	**6:45 or 5:27**

Act IV, sc. iii, lines 1-135 or 23-121 (prose)

Autolycus, pretending to have been robbed and beaten, picks the Clown's pocket as the Clown helps him. Autolycus sings.

(The Clown has only 1/3 of the lines. If Autolycus' song is cut, the scene is 5:27 minutes long and better balanced.)

SCENES FOR TWO WOMEN

Listed in alphabetical order, by play title, then in Act/scene order.

AS YOU LIKE IT	Celia/Rosalind	2:57

Act I, sc. ii, lines 1-59 (prose)

Celia comforts Rosalind, who is depressed by her father's exile: "Let us sit and mock the good housewife Fortune from her wheel, that her gifts may henceforth be bestowed equally."
(Rosalind has 32% of the lines, Celia 68%.)

AS YOU LIKE IT	Celia/Rosalind	2:06

Act I, sc. iii, lines 1-42 (prose)

Celia is amused that the forlorn Rosalind has fallen in love with Orlando at first sight: "Come, come, wrestle with thy affections."
Rosalind has only 17 lines (41%) but this is a good character scene.

AS YOU LIKE IT	Celia/Rosalind	2:27

Act I, sc. iii, lines 92-140 (verse)

Because Rosalind is banished from her uncle's court, she and Celia decide to flee to the forest of Arden disguised as brother and sister.
(Rosalind has 40% of the lines, Celia 60%.)

AS YOU LIKE IT	Celia/Rosalind	4:45

Act III, sc. ii, lines 172-266 (prose)

Celia tells the dumbfounded Rosalind that Orlando is the lovesick poet who is tacking love poems to all the trees.

AS YOU LIKE IT	Celia/Rosalind	12:15

Act I, sc. ii, lines 1-59; sc. iii, lines 1-42; lines 92-140 and Act III, sc. ii, lines 172-266

Combine these four scenes—described above—for an interesting character study of these two women.
(Bridging narration needed between the various scenes.)

CORIOLANUS	[Sicinius]/[Brutus]	4:08

Act II, sc. iii, lines 184-270 (verse)

Sicinius and Brutus, tribunes of the plebes, upbraid the people for acquiescing in the election of Coriolanus to the consulship, and instruct them how to get the election revoked.

(Both characters can be played by women; cut the Citizens' lines and the line tagged "All.")

HENRY V *Katharine/Alice* **3:12**

Act III, sc. iv, lines 1-64 (prose)

Expecting the English to defeat her father, the French princess, Katharine prepares to marry Henry V by learning English from her gentlewoman, Alice. The scene is written in French with a smattering of English.

(Alice has 38% of the lines, Katharine 62%.)

HENRY VIII *Anne/Old Lady* **3:48**

Act II, sc. iii, lines 1-49 & 81-107 (verse)

Anne Bullen and an Old Lady, her friend, talk about the estrangement between Queen Katharine and Henry VIII. The Old Lady doesn't believe that Anne would refuse the crown if it were offered.

Cut "Lo, who comes here?" from line 49; the Old Lady needs to carry a letter from Henry declaring Anne the Marchioness of Pembroke.

HENRY VIII *[Two Gentlemen]* **4:24**

Act II, sc. i, lines 1-54 & 136-169 (verse)

Two Gentlemen discuss the current events; Buckingham's trial and execution and Queen Katharine's imminent demise via Cardinal Wolsey.

(The two Gentlemen can be played as Gentlewomen.)

MERCHANT *Portia/Nerissa* **7:18**

Act I, sc. ii, lines 1-147 (prose)

Portia tells Nerissa, her waiting-maid, how her dead father's will dictates how a husband will be chosen for her. Nerissa enumerates Portia's suitors and Portia catalogues them.

(Incorporate the Servant's speech into Nerissa's part and cut the word, "Sirrah", in line 146. Nerissa has 32% of the lines, to Portia's 68%.

MERRY WIVES	**Mrs. Page/Mrs. Ford**	**5:36**

Act II, sc. i, lines 1-112 (prose)

Mrs. Ford and Mrs. Page have each received identical love letters from Falstaff and vow to get even with him. Comic prose dialogue for two mature women.
(Mrs. Ford has 1/3 of the lines, Mrs. Page has 2/3.)

MIDSUMMER	**[Puck/Fairy]**	**2:47**

Act II, sc. i, lines 1-59 (verse)

Puck and Fairy reveal the strife in the fairy kingdom and introduce themselves: "Over hill, over dale/Through bush, through brier."

OTHELLO	**Emilia/Desdemona**	**4:48 ✗**

Act IV, sc. iii, lines 11-106 (verse/prose)

Emilia commiserates with Desdemona over Othello's jealousy: the "willow" scene. Desdemona must sing.

ROMEO & JULIET	**Juliet/Nurse**	**4:00**

Act II, sc. v, lines 1-80 (verse)

Juliet worries why the Nurse is so long in returning from her meeting with Romeo. When the Nurse finally arrives, she would rather be pampered than tell her news.

ROMEO & JULIET	**Juliet/Nurse**	**5:30**

Act III, sc. ii, lines 34-143 (verse)

The Nurse leads Juliet to believe that Romeo is dead when she explains that Romeo killed Tybalt. The Nurse promises to bring the exiled Romeo to Juliet's bridal bed.
(The Nurse has 26% of the lines, Juliet has 74%.)

TWELFTH NIGHT	**Viola/Olivia**	**7:09**

Act I, sc. v, lines 174-330 (prose/verse)

Viola, disguised as a boy, woos Olivia for Orsino, but Olivia falls in love with Viola.
(Cut Maria's and Malvolio's lines, Viola's lines 217-220, and Olivia's lines 318-325.)

TWELFTH NIGHT   *Viola/[Feste*   **3:45**

Act III, sc. i, lines 1-76 (prose)

The Clown (Feste) and Viola discuss folly, language, and marriage.

(Feste can be played by a woman; change pronouns accordingly.)

TWELFTH NIGHT   *Viola/Olivia*   **3:54**

Act III, sc. i, lines 95-176 (verse)

Viola, disguised as a page, comes a second time to Olivia to plead her master, Orsino's suit. Olivia confesses love for Viola.

(Cut Sir Andrew's lines. Viola has 36% of the lines, Olivia has 64%.)

TWO GENTLEMEN   *Julia/Lucetta*   **7:00**

Act I, sc. ii, lines 1-140 (verse)

Lucetta angers Julia when she teases her about a love letter from Proteus to Julia which Lucetta has intercepted.

(Lucetta has 37% of the lines, Julia has 63%.)

TWO GENTLEMEN   *[Launce]/[Speed]*   **3:06**

Act II, sc. v, lines 1-62 (prose)

Two clowns, Launce and Speed, discuss their masters' mistresses.

(Both characters can be played by women.)

TWO GENTLEMEN   *Julia/Silvia*   **3:36**

Act IV, sc. iv, lines 113-184 (verse)

Disguised as a boy, Julia delivers Proteus' love letter to Silvia.

WINTER'S TALE   *[Archidamus/Camillo]*   **2:30**

Act I, sc. i, lines 1-50 (prose)

Archidamus of Bohemia and Camillo of Sicilia discuss the friendship of their kings and compliment each other's country. A characterless, prosy scene, but almost exactly balanced between the two roles.

SCENES FOR ONE MAN AND ONE WOMAN

Listed in alphabetical order by play title, then in Act/scene order.

ALL'S WELL	*Helena/Parolles*	7:09

Act I, sc. i, lines 109-244 (prose/verse)

Helena and Parolles discuss virginity: " 'Tis a commodity will lose the gloss with lying; the longer kept, the less worth."

(Begin with "Who comes here"; cut the Page's line. The opening aside and closing soliloquy help balance the parts.)

ALL'S WELL	*Helena/King*	5:36

Act II, sc. i, lines 102-213 (verse)

Helena offers to cure the King's illness. If she succeeds, he will bestow a husband on her; if she fails, she will die.

ALL'S WELL	*Diana/Bertram*	3:48

Act IV, sc. ii, lines 1-76 (verse)

Bertram woos Diana, offering his ring for her favors.

ANTONY & CLEO.	*Cleopatra/Antony*	4:38

Act I, sc. iii, lines 13-105 (verse)

Cleopatra quarrels with Antony when he tells her he must return to Rome because Fulvia is dead.

ANTONY & CLEO.	*Cleopatra/Antony*	2:59

Act IV, sc. xv, lines 9-68 (verse)

Antony dies; Cleopatra mourns: "I am dying Egypt, dying... "
(Cleopatra has 2/3 of the lines.)

COMEDY of ERRORS	*Lucinda/Antipholus of S.*	3:30

Act III, sc. ii, lines 1-70 (verse)

Luciana mistakes Antipholus of Syracuse for his brother and chides him for being strange with his wife, Adriana.

Antipholus responds by flirting with her. Rhyming quatrains and couplets.

CORIOLANUS	*Volumnia/Coriolanus*	9:45

Act V, sc. iii, lines 1-209 (verse)

Volumnia pleads with her son, Coriolanus, to spare Rome which he has resolved to destroy. There are other characters in the scene and it requires a performance style that makes their presence apparent.
(Cut Aufidius', Virgilia's and Marcius' lines.)

CORIOLANUS	*[Sicinius]/[Brutus]*	4:08

Act II, sc. iii, lines 184-270 (verse)

Sicinius and Brutus, tribunes of the plebes, upbraid the people for acquiescing in the election of Coriolanus to the consulship, and instruct them how to get the election revoked.
(Either character could be played by a woman. Cut the Citizens' lines and the line tagged "All.")

CYMBELINE	*Imogen/Iachimo*	10:22

Act I, sc. vi, lines 1-210 (verse)

Iachimo tries to seduce Imogen by telling her that her husband is false to her. She spurns him; he pretends to have been merely testing her and arranges to have himself secretly delivered to her bedroom in a trunk.
(Iachimo has 2/3 of the lines. Cut Pisanio's lines.)

CYMBELINE	*Imogen/Cloten*	2:54

Act II, sc. iii, lines 91-141, 154-161 (verse)

Imogen rebuffs Cloten's romantic advances. Cloten swears revenge after Imogen tells him that Posthumus, her husband's, "meanest garment...is dearer/In my respect than all the hairs above thee,/Were they all made such men."
(Cut "How now, Pisanio!" from line 141.)

CYMBELINE	*Imogen/Pisanio*	9:46

Act III, sc. iv, lines 1-195 (verse)

Pisanio tells Imogen that he has been ordered to kill her because his master, her husband, believes her to be unfaithful. Imogen grieves; Pisanio reveals a plan to save her.

| **HAMLET** | *Ophelia/Polonius* | **2:17** |

Act II, sc. i, lines 74-119 (verse)

Ophelia tells Polonius about Hamlet's strange behavior to her: "Lord Hamlet with his doublet all unbraced..."

| **HAMLET** | *Ophelia/Hamlet* | **4:04** |

Act III, sc. i, lines 88-169 (prose/verse)

Ophelia is abused by Hamlet in the "get thee to a nunnery" scene. Hamlet suspects that Polonius has put Ophelia up to returning gifts he gave her.
(Ophelia has 38% of the lines; Hamlet has 62%.)

| **HAMLET** | *Player Queen/Player King* | **3:42** |

Act III, sc. ii, lines 165-238 (verse)

The Player King and Player Queen perform the beginning of the "Murder of Gonzago," in rhymed couplets. A difficult, stylized scene, but certainly a challenge.

| **HAMLET** | *Gertrude/Hamlet* | **10:30 ✗** |

Act III, sc. iv, lines 8-217 (verse)

The closet scene. Hamlet upbraids Gertrude for having married Claudius and urges her to be continent. The scene involves the killing of Polonius behind a curtain, a problem that can be solved by using a third actor with two off-stage lines, by miming his presence, or by editing.

| **HENRY IV, Part I** | *Lady Percy/Hotspur* | **7:36** |

Act II, sc. iii, lines 1-68, 76-120 and Act III, sc. i, lines 229-267 (prose/verse)

Lady Percy insists, "Some heavy business hath my lord in hand,/And I must know it, else he loves me not." Hotspur, her husband, won't reveal his plans of rebellion against Henry IV. They quarrel, then say farewell. The second scene refers to background music.

| **HENRY IV, Part I** | *Mistress Quickly/Falstaff* | **2:06** |

Act III, sc. iii, lines 60-101 (prose)

Mistress Quickly presses Falstaff for payment of his bill, but Falstaff tries to dodge his debt by changing the subject to who picked his pocket. The actors need to be able to place Bardolph in the scene since they refer to him.

HENRY VI, Part I   *Joan/Charles*   3:43
Act I, sc. ii, lines 66-117, 127-150 (verse)

Joan La Pucelle (Joan of Arc) proves her power by defeating Charles, the Dauphin, in a fencing match. Both actors, but especially Joan, must fence.
(Charles has 32% of the lines; Joan has 68%. Charles takes Reignier's line 71; Joan takes Alencon's line 146. Cut Reignier's lines 147-148.)

HENRY VI, Part I   *Joan/Warwick[York]*   3:01
Act V, sc. iv, lines 34-93 (verse)

Joan La Pucelle (Joan of Arc) is condemned to the stake by York and Warwick. She pleads pregnancy but is condemned anyway.
(Warwick and York are combined into a single character.)

HENRY VI, Part I   *Margaret/Suffolk*   4:18
Act V, sc. iii, lines 45-130 (verse)

Suffolk courts Margaret for King Henry, but each discovers an attraction for the other. The scene has a large number of asides.
(Margaret has 28% of the lines; Suffolk has 72%.)

HENRY VI, Part II   *Duchess/Gloucester*   2:43
Act I, sc. ii, lines 1-55 (verse)

Gloucester and his wife, the Duchess, each reveal their dreams to each other. Gloucester dreams of overthrowing Somerset and Suffolk, but he warns the Duchess that her ambitious dreams are treasonous.

HENRY VI, Part II   *Duchess/Hume*   2:24
Act I, sc. ii, lines 60-107 (verse)

The Duchess of Gloucester reveals her ambition in a soliloquy and then pays Hume to set up a meeting with a witch

and a conjuror. Hume's soliloquy reveals his intentions of destroying the Duke and Duchess of Gloucester.
(Only a third of the scene is dialogue, with both actors present.)

HENRY VI, Part II	*Queen Margaret/Suffolk*	5:00

Act III, sc. ii, lines 300-366, 380-412 (verse)

Queen Margaret and the banished Suffolk bid a sorrowful goodbye to each other. The queen promises to lift his sentence of exile or to join him.

HENRY VI, Part III	*Lady Grey/Edward*	3:18

Act III, sc. ii, lines 36-106 (verse)

Lady Grey refuses King Edward's offer to regain her dead husband's confiscated lands by sleeping with him. He is so impressed with her charm and virtue that he offers to marry her.
(Cut Gloucester's and Clarence's lines.)

HENRY VIII	*Katherine/Griffith*	4:45

Act IV, sc. ii, lines 1-95 (verse)

Now the Princess Dowager instead of the queen, the sick Katharine speaks with her gentleman, Griffith, about Wolsey's demise. Katharine dreams about "spirits of peace."
(Cut the dream sequence.)

HENRY VIII	*[Two Gentlemen]*	4:24

Act II, sc. i, lines 1-54, 136-169 (verse)

Two Gentlemen discuss the current events: Buckingham's trial and executioin and Queen Katharine's imminent demise via Cardinal Wolsey.
(One of the gentlemen can be a gentlewoman.)

JULIUS CAESAR	*Calpurnia/Caesar*	2:27

Act II, sc. ii, lines 8-56 (verse)

Calpurnia begs Caesar to stay home because of several bad omens that have occurred during the night's storm: "When beggars die, there are no comets seen;/The heavens themselves blaze forth the death of princes."
(Incorporate the Servant's speech into Calpurnia's part.)

KING JOHN *[Arthur]/Hubert* 6:39

Act IV, sc. i, lines 1-135 (verse)

Arthur persuades Hubert, his keeper, not to burn his eyes out.

(Cut the Executioner's lines 6 and 86, but indicate his presence. Arthur can be played by a woman.)

KING LEAR *[Fool]/Lear* 2:21

Act I, sc. v, lines 8-56 (prose)

Lear and the Fool: "O, let me not be mad."

(The Fool can be played by a woman. Cut the Gentleman's line and Lear's line to him.)

KING LEAR *Cordelia/Lear* 2:35

Act IV, sc. vii, lines 26-84 (verse)

Lear and Cordelia are reunited.

(Cut Kent's and the Doctor's lines.)

KING LEAR *Regan/Lear* 3:00

Act II, sc. iv, lines 128-187 (verse)

Lear entreats Regan to shelter him and his men after Goneril has turned him away. The actor playing Lear must be able to place Kent.

(Incorporate Cornwall's lines into Regan.)

LOVE'S LABOURS *[Moth]/Armado* 6:27

Act I, sc. ii, lines 1-129 (prose)

Armado and Moth discuss Armado's love (unrequited) for Jacquenetta. Puns, chop-logic, and fantastical conceits.

(Moth can be played by a woman.)

MACBETH *Lady Macbeth/Macbeth* 4:06

Act I, sc. vii, lines 1-82 (verse)

Macbeth fears to kill Duncan, but Lady Macbeth strengthens his resolve.

MACBETH *Lady Macbeth/Macbeth* 3:43

Act II, sc. ii, lines 1-74 (verse)

Macbeth and Lady Macbeth murder Duncan.

(Macbeth has 38% of the lines; Lady Macbeth has 62%.)

MACBETH	*Lady Macbeth/Macbeth*	9:25

Act I, sc. vii, lines 1-82; Act II, sc. i, lines 31-64; and Act II, sc. ii, lines 1-74 (verse)

Lady Macbeth and Macbeth plotting to kill Duncan. Combine two scenes and Macbeth's dagger soliloquy for a longer piece.

MEASURE for MEASURE	*Isabell/Lucio*	3:49

Act I, sc. iv, lines 15-90 (verse)

Lucio tells Isabell that her brother, Claudio, is to be executed for lechery and urges her to work to secure his pardon.
(Lucio has 3/4 of the lines.)

MEASURE	*Isabell/Angelo*	7:25

Act II, sc. ii, lines 26-187 (verse)

Isabell pleads with Angelo for the life of her brother who is condemned to die for fornication. Angelo denies her, then tells her to come again, and at last admits (in a final soliloquy) that he feels lust for Isabell.
(Cut Lucio's and the Provost's asides as well as "Stay a little while" from line 26.)

MEASURE	*Isabell/Angelo*	8:24

Act II, sc. iv, lines 20-187 (verse)

Angelo, having condemned Claudio to death for fornication, tells Isabell, Claudio's sister, that he will spare Claudio in return for her sexual favors.

MEASURE	*Isabell/Angelo*	15:49

Act II, sc. ii, lines 26-187 and Act II, sc. iv, lines 20-187 (verse)

Combine the preceding scenes for a longer piece.

MEASURE	*Isabell/Claudio*	4:57

Act III, sc. i, lines 53-151 (verse)

Isabell tells Claudio, her brother, who is to die for fornication, that Angelo has offered to spare his life in exchange for her sexual favors, and that she has refused. Claudio greets the news with mixed feelings.

MERCHANT	*Jessica/Lorenzo*	2:50

Act II, sc. vi, lines 25-57 and Act V, sc. i, lines 1-24 (verse)

Disguised as a boy, Jessica elopes with Lorenzo. Then they trade love images: "In such a night as this..."

MERCHANT	*Portia/Bassanio*	9:21

Act III, sc. ii, lines 1-187 (verse)

Bassanio chooses the casket that gives Portia to him as his wife and swears never to part with the ring Portia gives to him. Portia sings the song, "Tell me where is fancy bred."

MERCHANT	*Portia/Bassanio*	3:17

Act III, sc. ii, lines 246-274, 294-330 (verse)

Bassanio receives a letter from Antonio regarding Antonio's bankruptcy. Portia tells Bassanio to go to Antonio's aid.

MERCHANT	*Portia/Bassanio*	2:03

Act IV, sc. i, lines 408-448 (verse)

Bassanio presses his thanks on the disguised Portia because she saved Antonio's life. Giving in to and testing Bassanio, she asks for the ring she gave to him and which he promised never to take off. Bassanio refuses, yet he feels ungrateful.

(Incorporate Antonio's lines into Bassanio's part.)

MERCHANT	*Portia/Shylock*	4:19

Act IV, sc. i, lines 176-179, 223-263, 298-347 (verse)

Disguised as a doctor of law, Portia turns Shylock's insistence on the letter of the law against him.

(Give Antonio's lines 243-244 to Shylock. Cut Gratiano's and Bassanio's lines.)

MERCHANT	*Portia/Bassanio*	2:57

Act V, sc. i, lines 184-233, 240-248 (verse)

Portia mercilessly teases Bassanio about the ring he gave to the "doctor of law" (Portia in disguise) as thanks for saving Antonio's life. Bassanio had promised never to part with the ring.

(Cut Nerissa's line.)

MERCHANT *Portia/Bassanio* **17:39**

Act III, sc. ii, 1-187; Act III, sc. ii, lines 246-274, 294-330; Act IV, sc. i, 408-448; and Act V, sc. i, 184-233, 240-248 (verse)

Combine all Portia and Bassanio scenes for a long piece.

MIDSUMMER *[Puck]/[Fairy]* **2:47**

Act II, sc. i, lines 1-59 (verse)

Puck and Fairy reveal the strife in the fairy kingdom and introduce themselves: "Over hill, over dale/Through bush, through brier."

(Either Puck or the Fairy can be played by a woman.)

MIDSUMMER *Hermia/Lysander* **2:36**

Act I, sc. i, lines 128-179 (verse)

Hermia and Lysander plan to elope because her father insists she marry Demetrius.

MIDSUMMER *Helena/Demetrius* **2:51**

Act II, sc. i, lines 188-244 (verse)

Helena, in love with Demetrius, follows after him; he in turn follows after Hermia (whom he loves), who is eloping with Lysander.

MIDSUMMER *Helena/Lysander* **2:52**

Act II, sc. ii, lines 88-144 (verse)

Lysander awakens and–because he has a love potion on his eyes–instantly falls in love with Helena and out of love with the sleeping Hermia.

MIDSUMMER *Hermia/Demetrius* **2:15**

Act III, sc. ii, lines 43-87 (verse)

Demetrius pleads his love to Hermia, who, looking for Lysander and thinking Demetrius has killed him, will have nothing to do with him.

(Demetrius has only 17 lines–38%.)

MIDSUMMER *[Puck]/Oberon* **6:22**

Act III, sc. ii, lines 1-42, 88-121, 345-400 (verse)

Puck has satisfactorily carried out Oberon's trick upon Titania but has failed Oberon's good intentions toward the four lovers. Oberon commands him to set things straight. The scene requires the imagined presence of the lovers. *(Puck can be played by a woman.)*

MUCH ADO	*Beatrice/Benedick*	**1:39**

Act I, sc. i, lines 114-146 (prose)

The first glimpse of the "merry war" between Beatrice and Benedick. This "skirmish of wit" foreshadows their falling in love with each other.

MUCH ADO	*Beatrice/Benedick*	**4:12**

Act IV, sc. i, lines 257-340 (verse)

When Benedick and Beatrice finally admit their love for one another, Beatrice demands that Benedick kill Claudio for slandering Hero's virtue.

MUCH ADO	*Beatrice/Benedick*	**2:45**

Act V, sc. ii, lines 42-96 (prose)

Beatrice comes to Benedick after he has challenged Claudio. Another feisty courtship scene between them during which they agree that they "are too wise to woo peaceably."

MUCH ADO	*Beatrice/Benedick*	**8:36**

Act I, sc. i, lines 114-146; Act IV, sc. i, lines 257-340; and Act V, sc. ii, lines 42-96 (prose)

Combine the scenes described above for one long piece— the entire love war between Beatrice and Benedick.

OTHELLO	*Desdemona/Othello*	**3:12**

Act III, sc. iii, lines 41-92, 278-289 (verse)

Desdemona pleads with Othello to see Cassio so that Othello will forgive Cassio of his drunken brawl. Othello's jealousy begins to surface. Desdemona drops her handkerchief when she tries to bind Othello's brow.
(Othello has only 20 lines.)

OTHELLO	*Desdemona/Othello*	**3:19**

Act III, sc. iv, lines 33-98 (verse)

Othello asks Desdemona for the handkerchief he gave her; Desdemona talks of Cassio, which increases Othello's jealousy.
(Othello has 2/3 of the lines.)

OTHELLO	Desdemona/Othello	4:42

Act V, sc. ii, lines 1-100 (verse)
Othello kills Desdemona.
(Cut Emilia's off-stage lines; cut Othello's lines 89 and 91-93. Desdemona has 37% of the lines; Othello has 63%.

OTHELLO	Desdemona/Othello	11:13

Act III, sc. iii, lines 41-92, 278-289; Act III, sc. iv, lines 33-98; and Act V, sc. ii, lines 1-100 (verse)
The sequence of Othello's growing jealousy, unknowingly fed by Desdemona, leading to his killing her.
(Combine preceding scenes for a long piece.)

PERICLES	Dionyzia/Cleon	2:33

Act IV, sc. iii, lines 1-51 (verse)
Dionyzia admits to Cleon that she had Marina murdered because Marina excelled Dionyzia's daughter.
(Dionyzia had 2/3 of the lines.)

RICHARD II	Queen/Gardener	2:00

Act III, sc. iv, lines 67-107 (verse)
The Queen learns from the Gardener that the king will be deposed.
(The Gardener starts with the second half of the Servant's line 67: "The King shall be deposed." Cut the question mark.)

RICHARD II	Queen/Richard	4:03

Act V, sc. i, lines 1-50, 71-102 (verse)
A parting scene in which the deposed King Richard on his way to internment meets his Queen for the last time. They say goodbye to each other.
(Cut Northumberland's line 84.)

RICHARD III	Lady Anne/Richard	9:24 X

Act I, sc. ii, lines 33-37, 43-225 (verse)

Richard, as yet Duke of Gloucester, woos and wins Lady Anne whose father, father-in-law, and husband he has helped kill.

RICHARD III Queen Elizabeth/Richard 3:54

Act I, sc. iii, lines 42-53, 62-91, 103-110, 113-154 (verse)

Richard, as yet Duke of Gloucester, protests that Queen Elizabeth is spreading rumors that he dislikes her and her followers. She protests his accusations.

(From lines 113-154, cut Queen Margaret's and River's speeches as well as Duke of Gloucester's last speech.)

RICHARD III *Queen Elizabeth/Richard* 11:48

Act IV, sc. iv, lines 196-431 (verse)

King Richard convinces Queen Elizabeth to woo her daughter for him.

ROMEO & JULIET *Juliet/Romeo* 9:28 ✗

Act II, sc. ii, lines 1-190 (verse)

The balcony scene: Romeo and Juliet profess their love to each other and make plans to marry.

(Cut the Nurse's off-stage lines.)

ROMEO & JULIET *Nurse/Romeo* 3:00

Act II, sc. iv, lines 170-229 (prose)

The Nurse meets Romeo to set the time of his wedding to Juliet.

(Romeo has 1/3 of the lines; the Nurse has 2/3.)

ROMEO & JULIET *Juliet/Romeo* 3:08

Act III, sc. v, lines 1-64 (verse)

On the morning after their wedding night, Romeo and Juliet part.

(There are three lines for the Nurse: 37, 39, 40. Line 37 can be cut; Juliet can take lines 39 and 40, changing "your" to "my.")

ROMEO & JULIET *Juliet/Fr. Laurence* 4:07

Act IV, sc. i, lines 44-126 (verse)

Juliet threatens suicide if Friar Laurence doesn't help her rejoin Romeo in Mantua. Friar Laurence offers her a drug which will help her feign death.

TAMING of the SHREW *Katharina/Petruchio* 5:30 ✗

Act II, sc. i, lines 169-282 (verse)

Katharina meets Petruchio for the first time and a confrontation of strong wills begins, expressed largely in punning repartee and quick exchange of short lines.

THE TEMPEST *Miranda/Ferdinand* 4:25

Act III, sc. i, lines 1-91 (verse)

Ferdinand, set to work by Prospero, is pitied by Miranda. They fall in love.

(Cut Prospero's asides.)

THE TEMPEST *[Ariel]/Prospero* 5:54

Act I, sc. ii, lines 187-304 (verse)

Ariel tells Porspero how she staged the shipwreck and begs her freedom. Prospero calls her ungrateful and reminds her of her obligations to Prospero.

(Ariel can be played by a woman.)

TITUS ANDRONICUS *Tamora/Aaron* 2:42

Act II, sc. iii, lines 1-54 (verse)

A love scene in which Aaron and Tamora plot Bassianus' death and Lavinia's rape.

(Basically one long speech for each. Tamora has 37% of the lines; Aaron has 61%.)

TITUS ANDRONICUS *Tamora/Titus* 7:09

Act V, sc. ii, lines 1-148 (verse)

Tamora, disguised as Revenge, tries to fool Titus and shape his plans to her advantage.

(Cut Demetrius', Chiron's, and Marcus' lines. The actors must suggest the presence of these characters.)

TROILUS & CRESSIDA *Cressida/Pandarus* 13:45

Act I, sc. ii, lines 43-321 (prose)

Pandarus and Cressida watch the Trojan heroes return from battle. Pandarus praises Troilus, saying he excells them. Cressida pretends to dislike him, but then, in a brief verse soliloquy, admits she loves him.

(Cut Pandarus' and the Boy's lines 297-301 and the first sentence in line 302.)

TROILUS & CRESSIDA   *[Servant]/Pandarus*   **2:15**

Act III, sc. i, lines 1-45 (prose)

   Pandarus seeks information from Paris' Servant: "Friend, we understand not one another; I am too courtly, and thou art too cunning."

TROILUS & CRESSIDA   *Cressida/Troilus*   **6:10**

Act III, sc. ii, lines 64-106, 121-214 (prose/verse)

   Troilus and Cressida are finally brought together by Pandarus. They declare their love for and fidelity to each other. The "true as Troilus," "false as Cressida" scene.

(Cut Pandarus' lines.)

TWELFTH NIGHT   *Viola/Captain*   **3:00**

Act I, sc. ii, lines 1-64 (verse)

   Viola, rescued at sea by the Captain, is brought to Illyria and resolves to serve Orsino as a page. The Captain describes the country and its duke.

TWELFTH NIGHT   *Maria/Sir Toby Belch*   **2:18**

Act I, sc. iii, lines 1-46 (prose)

   Maria chides Sir Toby Belch: "That quaffing and drinking will undo you." They discuss Sir Andrew, "a very fool and a prodigal."

TWELFTH NIGHT   *Maria/Feste*   **2:00**

Act I, sc. v, lines 1-40 (prose)

   Maria tells the Clown, Feste, that "my lady will hang thee for thy absence." Feste jokes about it and concludes, "Better a witty fool than a foolish wit."

TWELFTH NIGHT   *Viola/Orsino*   **3:40**

Act II, sc. iv, lines 15-42, 82-127 (verse)

   The Duke, Orsino, asks Viola (disguised as a boy, his page) if "he" has ever loved as Orsino loves Olivia. Viola describes an imaginary lover, who is in fact Orsino, and describes an imaginary sister, in fact herself, who "sat like patience on a monument,/Smiling at grief."

TWELFTH NIGHT	*Viola/Feste*	3:45

Act III, sc. i, lines 1-75 (prose)
   The Clown (Feste) and Viola discuss folly, language, and marriage.

TWELFTH NIGHT	*Malvolio/[Feste]*	6:09

Act IV, sc. ii, lines 1-141 (prose)
   Malvolio has been imprisoned in a dark room because his enemies have tricked him and convinced Olivia he is mad. The Clown, Feste, comes to him as "Sir Topas," the curate, who is to restore his sanity and later, speaks as himself.
   (Feste can be played by a woman. Edit opening speeches thus: Feste: "I'll put on this gown and this beard; make him believe I am Sir Topas the curate." Then Feste's own speech, cutting the last sentance, and then going into "for as the old hermit..." in line 13. Then play the scene as written, cutting Toby's and Maria's lines.)

TWO GENTLEMEN	*[Speed]/Proteus*	4:36

Act I, sc. i, lines 70-161 (prose)
   Proteus asks Speed if he has delivered a love letter to Julia. Speed misconstrues and puns at all the questions.
   (Speed can be played by a woman.)

TWO GENTLEMEN	*[Speed]/Valentine*	4:54

Act II, sc. i, lines 1-98 (prose)
   Valentine plays straight man to his servant, Speed, as they discuss Silvia, Valentine's new love.
   (Speed can be played by a woman.)

TWO GENTLEMEN	*[Launce]/[Speed]*	3:06

Act II, sc. v, lines 1-62 (prose)
   Two clowns, Launce and Speed, discuss their masters' mistresses.
   (Either part can be played by a woman.)

TWO GENTLEMEN	*Launce/[Speed]*	5:51

Act III, sc. i, lines 279-395 (prose)

A clown scene: Launce and Speed mull over a love letter itemizing the virtues of Launce's love.
(Speed can be played by a woman.)

WINTER'S TALE	*[Archidamus]/[Camillo]*	2:30

Act I, sc. i, lines 1-50 (prose)
Archidamus of Bohemia and Camillo of Sicilia discuss the friendship of their kings and compliment each other's country.
(A characterless, prosy scene, but almost exactly balanced between the two roles, and either character can be played by a woman.)

WINTER'S TALE	*Hermione/Leontes*	3:31

Act II, sc. i, lines 56-125 (verse)
Leontes accuses his wife, Hermione, of infidelity. Hermione is pregnant.

WINTER'S TALE	*Paulina/Leontes*	4:37

Act III, sc. ii, lines 149-244 (verse)
Leontes learns from Paulina that Hermione, his wife, has died of grief after being accused of adultery and hearing of her son's death. Paulina curses him, and he mourns. Good vituperation and anguish.
(Cut the 1st Lord's lines 217-219 and Paulina's lines 219-220. Leontes takes the balance of the 1st Lord's lines.)

WINTER'S TALE	*Perdita/Florizel*	2:43

Act IV, sc. iv, lines 1-54 (verse)
Florizel, a prince dressed as a shepherd and Perdita (who thinks herself a shepherdess), dressed as a goddess, await guests at a rural festivity. She is embarrassed by her costume, he reassures her, and they pledge their love.

SCENES FOR THREE ACTORS

Listed in alphabetical order by play title, then in Act/scene order.

AS YOU LIKE IT	3M		3:54

Act II, sc. vii, lines 62-139 (verse)

ORLANDO, with sword drawn, intrudes on a discussion between JAQUES and DUKE SENIOR about Jaques' faults. Desperate for food for Adam, Orlando is taken aback by the generosity of the two men whom he thinks are outlaws.

COMEDY OF ERRORS	2M, 1W	4:51

Act IV, sc. iii, lines 1-97 (prose/verse)

ANTIPHOLUS and DROMIO OF SYRACUSE, confused about being recognized in Ephesus, are met by the COURTEZAN, who invites Antipholus to dinner.

CORIOLANUS	3W	6:12

Act I, sc. iii, lines 1-124 (prose)

VOLUMNIA, VIRGILIA and VALERIA discuss Coriolanus. Volumnia and Valeria express the stock Roman matron's view of heroism; Virgilia fears that Coriolanus will be killed or injured.

(Volumnia has 43% of the lines, Virgilia 20%; Virgilia takes the Gentlewoman's line 29.)

CORIOLANUS	3M [3W; 1M,2W; 2M,1W]	4:54

Act IV, sc. v, lines 154-251 (prose)

THREE SERVANTS discuss the defection of Coriolanus to the Volscian side. A colloquial, gossipy scene.

(Any or all of the servants could be played by women.)

HAMLET	3M	6:00 *or* 7:60

Act I, sc. i, lines 18-175 (verse)

BERNARDO, MARCELLUS, and HORATIO see the Ghost of King Hamlet.

(Bernardo has 15%, Horatio 62%; a shorter (6:00) cutting with better balance can be had by cutting lines 70-107, so Bernardo has

20%, Horatio, 57%. The balance could be improved still further by assigning Bernardo one of Horatio's longer speeches.)

| **HAMLET** | **2M, 1W** | **6:48** |

Act I, sc. iii, lines 1-136 (verse)

    LAERTES and POLONIUS counsel OPHELIA to beware of Hamlet's attentions. The scene contains Polonius' "to thine own self be true," a fearful chestnut, which could be shortened to improve the balance.

(Ophelia has 15% of the lines; Polonius has 47%.)

| **HAMLET** | **3M** | **13:30** |

Act II, sc. ii, lines 170-439 (prose)

    POLONIUS, then ROSENCRANTZ/GUILDENSTERN, question and spy on HAMLET. Discussion of the theatre and the Elizabethan boys' companies.

(Polonius has 16% of the lines; Hamlet has 62%. Combine Rosencrantz and Guildenstern into one character, cutting names and changing pronouns where necessary. Cut line 300.)

| **HENRY IV, Part I** | **3M** | **12:00 or 7:36** |

Act I, sc. ii, lines 1-240 or lines 65-217 (prose)

    PRINCE HAL and FALSTAFF discuss thievery and Falstaff's hope that when Hal becomes king he will hang no thieves. POINS comes in and tells of a plan to rob some pilgrims. Falstaff leaves and Poins says he and Hal will betray Falstaff after the robbery, and steal from him. Poins leaves and Hal tells us he will drop his friends when he is king.

(The balance is poor: Poins has only 22% of the lines, Hal 40%. If the scene is played from lines 65-217, which plays 7:36, the balance is excellent.)

| **HENRY IV, Part I** | **3M** | **9:30** |

Act III, sc. i, lines 1-190 (verse)

    Much to HOTSPUR'S annoyance, GLENDOWER boasts of the supernatural marvels at his birth. MORTIMER tries to placate Glendower and warns Hotspur not to push their ally into abandoning them.

(Mortimer takes Worcester's one speech.)

HENRY IV, Part I	2M, 1W	8:30

Act III, sc. iii, lines 60-230 (prose)

FALSTAFF accuses MISTRESS QUICKLY of allowing him to be robbed in her house. They quarrel and PRINCE HAL arbitrates. Then he tells Falstaff he has procured for him an infantry command.

(Quickly takes Bardolph's lines. Cut "Bardolph" from line 160.)

HENRY IV, Part I	2M, 1W	4:44

Act III, sc. iii, lines 102-196 (prose)

PRINCE HAL arbitrates a quarrel between FALSTAFF and MISTRESS QUICKLY regarding Falstaff's debts and a charge of pickpocketing. Falstaff loses.

(A shortened version of the above cited scene. Quickly takes Bardolph's lines. Cut the word "Bardolph" from line 160.)

HENRY IV, Part I	3M	5:54

Act V, sc. i, lines 1-20 (verse)

WORCESTER, KING HENRY, and PRINCE HAL meet at the king's camp near Shrewsbury to try to avert an impending civil war. Worcester states his grievances against the king. Hal says he will meet Hotspur in single combat and so save bloodshed on both sides. King Henry declines Hal's offer and offers amnesty to the rebels if they'll put down their arms.

(Cut Prince Hal's and Falstaff's lines 28 and 29.)

HENRY IV, Part II	3M	5:30

Act I, sc. iii, lines 1-110 (verse)

The ARCHBISHOP OF YORK confers with HASTINGS and LORD BARDOLPH about their chances in continuing the rebellion against King Henry.

(Hastings takes Mowbray's lines 5-9 and 109. Change the word "Marshall" in line 4 to "Hastings.")

HENRY IV, Part II	2M, 1W	4:40

Act II, sc. i, lines 50-144 (prose)

MISTRESS QUICKLY attacks FALSTAFF when he insults her. The LORD CHIEF JUSTICE arbitrates the matter of

Falstaff's indebtedness to Mistress Quickly as well as his breach of promise.
(Cut Fang's lines 48-49.)

HENRY IV, Part II   3M   **11:05**

Act IV, sc. i, lines 1-228 (verse)

WESTMORELAND, as envoy from Prince John, asks the ARCHBISHOP OF YORK and MOWBRAY what their grievances are against King Henry. Westmoreland asks them to meet with Prince John so that they may outline terms of a peace.
(The Archbishop takes Hastings' lines 186-189; Mowbray takes the rest of Hastings' lines. Cut from Hastings' line 18 through Mowbray's line 24.)

HENRY IV, Part II   3M   **4:36**

Act V, sc. i, lines 1-98 (prose)

FALSTAFF visits JUSTICE SHALLOW in order to make a fool of him; Shallow tells his servant, DAVY, to make Falstaff comfortable because "a friend i' the court is better than a penny in the purse."
(Cut lines 60-65, "come, come...fellow.")

HENRY V   3M   **4:33**

Act III, sc. vi, lines 1-91 (prose/verse)

PISTOL begs FLUELLEN and GOWER for mercy for Bardolph, who is to be hanged. Fluellen refuses; he and Gower express their disappointment in Pistol. Fluellen uses a Welsh dialect.
(Pistol has 23% of the lines, Fluellen 52%.)

HENRY V   3M   **8:27**

Act III, sc. vii, lines 1-169 (prose)

The CONSTABLE OF FRANCE, the DUKE OF OR-LEANS, and the DAUPHIN anxiously wait for the morning to come so that they may engage the English in battle at Agincourt. They boast of their armor and horses. The two lords gossip about the Dauphin and pity the English.
Orleans takes both Rambures' and the Messenger's lines.

HENRY V	**3M [2M, 1W]**	**4:06**

Act IV, sc. iv, lines 1-82 (prose)

PISTOL encounters a FRENCH SOLDIER whom he captures with the help of the BOY'S French translating abilities. The Soldier speaks French; the Boy speaks both French and English.

(The Soldier has 22% of the lines; the Boy has 40%. The Boy could be played by a woman.)

HENRY V	**3M**	**4:43**

Act V, sc. i, lines 1-94 (prose)

For revenge, FLUELLEN forces the feisty PISTOL to eat a leek. GOWER backs up Fluellen.

(Gower has 19% of the lines, Fluellen 55%.)

HENRY V	**3M**	**9:15**

Act III, sc. vi, lines 1-91 and Act V, sc. i, lines 1-94 (prose/verse)

FLUELLEN, PISTOL and GOWER in a combination of two previously cited scenes.

(Narration will have to be provided to bridge the two scenes. Balance is not good, with Fluellen having more than 1/2 of the lines.)

HENRY VI, Part I	**2M, 1W**	**4:39**

Act V, sc. iv, lines 1-93 (verse)

JOAN LA PUCELLE (Joan of Arc) denies and reviles the SHEPHERD, her father, and is condemned to burn by YORK/WARWICK. She pleads pregnancy but is condemned anyway.

(York and Warwick are combined into a single role.)

HENRY VI, Part III	**3M**	**4:42**

Act II, sc. i, lines 1-94 (verse)

EDWARD and RICHARD learn of their father, the Duke of York's, death after witnessing three suns rising at dawn and combining into a single star. The MESSENGER recounts the death.

(The Messenger has 22% of the lines, Richard 45%.)

HENRY VI, Part III   3M   4:09

Act II, sc. v, lines 1-13, 55-124 (verse)

Near a battlefield, KING HENRY observes a SON who has just killed his father and a FATHER who has just killed his son. There is no interchange between the characters: the scene is virtually a set of short soliloquies. Two bodies must be provided or suggested.

(The Son has 26% of the lines, Henry 40%.)

HENRY VI, Part III   3M   4:00

Act II, sc. vi, lines 31-110 (verse)

WARWICK, RICHARD, and EDWARD find Clifford's corpse on the battlefield and know that they have beaten Queen Margaret. Edward makes Richard the Duke of Gloucester and Warwick sets off to France to bring Edward back a wife and queen. The corpse of Clifford must be suggested or provided.

(Edward takes George's lines.)

HENRY VIII   3M   3:21

Act I, sc. iii, lines 1-67 (verse)

The LORD CHAMBERLAIN and LORD SANDS learn from SIR THOMAS LOVELL that the dandified young fops returned from France are banned from court. They also talk of the generosity of Wolsey.

HENRY VIII   3M   5:57

Act III, sc. ii, lines 228-332, 337-350 (verse)

SURREY and SUFFOLK demand that WOLSEY give up the great seal of England.

(Suffolk takes all of Norfolk's lines.)

JULIUS CAESAR   2M, 1W   5:09

Act II, sc. ii, lines 1-3, 8-107 (verse)

CALPURNIA tries to dissuade CAESAR from going to the capitol, but DECIUS comes in and persuades him to go.

(Caesar has 50% of the lines, the remainder evenly divided between Calpurnia and Decius. Calpurnia takes the Servant's lines 38-40.)

KING LEAR	3M [2M, 1W]	4:48

Act III, sc. ii, lines 1-96 (verse)

LEAR, the FOOL, and KENT on the heath in the storm: "Blow, winds, and crack your cheeks."

(Kent has 16% of the lines; Lear has 58%. A slight improvement in balance could be achieved by inserting the first five lines of III, iv, between lines 78 and 79. Kent would now have 21% of the lines. The Fool could be played by a woman.)

KING LEAR	3M	9:33

Act IV, sc. vi, lines 1-191 (verse/prose)

EDGAR, disguised, leads GLOUCESTER, blind, to Dover. He makes him think he has survived a leap from the cliffs. LEAR, mad, enters and raves.

Gloucester has 23% of the lines, Lear 46%.

LOVE'S LABOUR'S	3M [2M, 1W]	7:09

Act III, sc. i, lines 1-143 (prose)

ARMADO, MOTH, and COSTARD in an almost content-less scene of word play, quibbles, and "sweet smoke of rhetoric."

(Costard has 19% of the lines. Moth could be played by a woman.)

MACBETH	3M	4:07

Act IV, sc. iii, lines 159-240 (verse)

ROSS brings to MACDUFF and MALCOLM the news of the massacre of Macduff's family. "All my pretty chickens and their dam/In one fell swoop."

MACBETH	1M,2W	4:20 ✗

Act V, sc. i, lines 1-87 (prose)

The sleepwalking scene: LADY MACBETH, DOCTOR, GENTLEWOMAN.

MERCHANT	2M, 1W	4:45

Act III, sc. v, lines 1-95 (prose/verse)

LAUNCELOT teases JESSICA about her father's sins being visited upon her. Launcelot bandies words with LORENZO about getting dinner prepared. A clown scene.

MERRY WIVES	**1M,2W**	**7:48**

Act III, sc. iii, lines 1-156 (prose)

The basket scene: with MRS. PAGE'S help, MRS. FORD pretends love for FALSTAFF, then has him hide in a laundry basket to avoid detection by her husband, and has the basket thrown into a ditch.

(The scene requires a basket and two non-speaking servants to carry it. Robin must be cut from the scene or one of the servants could take his few lines.)

MIDSUMMER	**1M,2W**	**6:12**

Act I, sc. i, lines 128-251 (verse)

LYSANDER and HERMIA plan to elope. HELENA is happy for them because Demetrius will then be free for Helena to woo, even though Demetrius loves Hermia. Partly in rhyming couplets.

MUCH ADO	**2M, 1W [1M, 2W]**	**4:42**

Act I, sc. i, lines 1-95 (prose)

A MESSENGER brings news of the successful war to LEONATO, Governor of Messina, and his niece, BEATRICE. He tells of the honorable deeds of two young lords, Claudio and Benedick, who fought in the war. Beatrice makes jokes about Benedick.

(Cut Leonato's line 34 and give Leonato Hero's line 35, adjusting the line to read, "My niece means Signior Benedick of Padua." The Messenger could be played by a woman.)

MUCH ADO	**3M**	**8:24**

Act I, sc. i, lines 163-330 (prose)

CLAUDIO, who is in love with Hero but doesn't know what to do about it, asks the advice of BENEDICK and DON PEDRO. Benedick says he is against women and marriage. Don Pedro offers to find out Hero's feelings by disguising himself as Claudio.

MUCH ADO	3W	4:45

Act III, sc. iv, lines 1-98 (prose)

MARGARET teases HERO about Claudio and BEATRICE about Benedick on the occasion of Hero's wedding morning. *(The balance is poor: Hero has 19% of the lines, Margaret 59%. Cut Ursula's lines 3 & 5, Beatrice takes Ursula's lines 95-97 and cut "good Ursula" from Hero's line 99.)*

MUCH ADO	3M	5:00

Act V, sc. i, lines 110-209 (prose)

BENEDICK challenges CLAUDIO to a duel to avenge Hero. Claudio and DON PEDRO don't take the challenge seriously and tease him about being in love with Beatrice.

OTHELLO	3M	9:12

Act I, sc. i, lines 1-184 (verse)

The opening scene: IAGO and RODERIGO express their hatred of Othello and rouse BRABANTIO from his bed to tell him his daughter has eloped with the Moor. *(Roderigo has 22% of the lines; Iago, 55%.)*

RICHARD II	3M	9:24

Act I, sc. i, lines 15-205 (verse)

BOLINGBROOKE and MOWBRAY accuse each other of treason. KING RICHARD tries, unsuccessfully to pacify them and finally decides to allow a trial by combat. *(Cut Richard's lines 158-159 and Gaunt's line 160. Richard takes Gaunt's other lines, 161-163, but change "my son" and "Harry" to "cousin.")*

RICHARD II	3M	8:00

Act I, sc. iii, lines 7-207 (verse)

By order of KING RICHARD, BOLINGBROOKE and MOWBRAY prepare for trial by combat, each maintaining his own loyalty and the treason of the other. At the last moment Richard cancels the combat and banishes both men. *(Cut all the lines of all other characters and cut Bolingbrooke's lines 84 and 102.)*

RICHARD II　　　　3M　　　　　　　17:24

Act I, sc. i, lines 15-205 and Act I, sc. iii, lines 7-207 (verse)
　　BOLINGBROOKE, MOWBRAY and KING RICHARD, in a combination of the above cited scenes.

RICHARD III　　　　3M　　　　　　　9:30

Act I, sc. iv, lines 101-290 (prose/verse)
　　Two MURDERERS who are hired by Gloucester first balk at killing CLARENCE, then, with the thought of money, stab him and drown him in a butt of malmsey despite his entreaties.

ROMEO & JULIET　　　3M [2M, 1W]　　　3:27

Act I, sc. ii, lines 38-106 (verse/prose)
　　A SERVANT encounters ROMEO and BENVOLIO and asks them to read an invitation list for a Capulet party. Romeo and Benvolio decide to crash the party.
(The Servant could be played by a woman.)

ROMEO & JULIET　　　1M,2W　　　　　7:18

Act III, sc. v, lines 60-205 (verse)
　　CAPULET and LADY CAPULET insist that JULIET marry Paris. Juliet refuses and incurs her father's wrath.
(Incorporate the Nurse's lines into Lady Capulet's role.)

TAMING of the SHREW　3M　　　　　7:00

Act I, sc. ii, lines 1-140 (verse)
　　Petruchio, attended by Grumio, visits Hortensio, who persuades him to woo and wed "Katharine the curst."

TAMING of the SHREW　3M　　　　　4:21

Act II, sc. i, lines 327-413 (verse)
　　The young TRANIO and the old GREMIO argue over who will wed BAPTISTA'S daughter, Bianca.
(Baptista has 22% of the lines, the rest are divided evenly between Tranio and Gremio.)

TAMING of the SHREW 2M, 1W   4:27

Act III, sc. i, lines 1-92 (verse/prose)

LUCENTIO, disguised as a tutor, and HORTENSIO, disguised as a music-master, vie for the love of BIANCA.
(Cut the Servant's lines 82-84)

TEMPEST   3M   9:36

Act II, sc. ii, lines 1-192 (prose)

CALIBAN hides from TRINCULO by playing dead. Trinculo takes refuge from the storm under Caliban's cloak. STEPHANO, drunk, thinks he has found a two-headed monster. Trinculo and Stephano get Caliban drunk and tame him. A beautiful low comedy scene.

TIMON of ATHENS   3M   5:55

Act V, sc. i, lines 1-118 (prose/verse)

The POET and the PAINTER, hearing that TIMON has gold, come to him to flatter him, but are driven off.

TITUS ANDRONICUS   3M   3:32

Act II, sc. i, lines 25-135 (verse)

DEMETRIUS and CHIRON almost come to blows over Lavinia until AARON persuades them to rape her, and thus share her.
(Aaron has 55% of the lines.)

TROILUS & CRESSIDA 3M   6:48

Act II, sc. i, lines 1-142 (prose)

Raillery, insults, and beatings between THERSITES, AJAX, and ACHILLES.
(Basically Thersites' scene: he has 60% of the lines, the others 20% each.)

TROILUS & CRESSIDA   2M,1W   6:15

Act III, sc. i, lines 46-172 (prose)

PANDARUS, PARIS, and HELEN in a scene of banter, puns, innuendo. Engaging, but not Shakespeare's best wit. Pandarus must sing.
(Helen and Paris each have 25% of the lines; Pandarus has 50%.)

TROILUS & CRESSIDA   2M, 1W   10:39
Act III, sc. ii, lines 8-220 (prose/verse)

 PANDARUS brings TROILUS and CRESSIDA together, and sends them off to bed. Lyric, erotic, and bawdy. The "true as Troilus"—"false as Cressid" scene.

TROILUS & CRESSIDA   2M, 1W   6:42
Act IV, sc. ii, lines 76-115 and Act IV, sc. iii, lines 13-110 (prose/verse)

 PANDARUS brings the news to TROILUS and CRESSIDA that they must part because she has been exchanged for a Trojan prisoner of the Greeks. The lovers grieve and swear to be faithful.

(Pandarus has 25% of the lines; Troilus has 41%. Cut the off-stage lines of Aeneas and Paris.)

TROILUS & CRESSIDA   2M, 1W   19:33
Act III, sc. ii, lines 8-220; Act IV, sc. ii, lines 1-44, 76-115; and Act IV, sc. iii, lines 13-110 (prose/verse)

 The bringing together of TROILUS and CRESSIDA by PANDARUS and their forced separation. A combination of two scenes cited above and the first 44 lines of Act IV, sc. iii.

(Narration will have to be provided to bridge the scenes; Pandarus should be the narrator.)

TWELFTH NIGHT   2M, 1W   7:33
Act I, sc. iii, lines 1-151 (prose)

 SIR TOBY introduces SIR ANDREW to MARIA. She chides Toby for drinking and resists Andrew's advances. Toby teases Andrew—who is unaware of being teased.

(Maria has 21% of the lines, Toby has 45%.)

TWELFTH NIGHT   3M [2M, 1W]   3:45
Act II, sc. iii, lines 1-75 (prose)

 SIR TOBY, SIR ANDREW, and the Clown, FESTE, drink and sing. Feste should sing well; he has the song, "O Mistress Mine."

(Feste could be played by a woman.)

TWELFTH NIGHT	**2M,1W [1M,2W]**	**6:21**

Act II, sc. iv, lines 1-127(verse)

The CLOWN, Feste, sings "Come away, death" to the DUKE ORSINO, and VIOLA, disguised as a page. Orsino talks of his love for Olivia; Viola, cryptically, talks of her love for Orsino. This is perhaps the most lyrical scene in Shakespeare.

(Feste, who must be a singer, could be played by a woman; has only 20% of lines. Viola takes Curio's lines.)

TWO GENTLEMEN	**2M,1W [1M,2W]**	**4:30**

Act II, sc. i, lines 102-191 (verse/prose)

SILVIA flirts with VALENTINE. SPEED enjoys Silvia's cleverness about a letter and teases Valentine about her coyness.

(Speed could be played by a woman.)

TWO GENTLEMEN	**3M**	**5:27**

Act III, sc. i, lines 170-278 (verse/prose)

After learning that his actions have caused VALENTINE'S banishment, PROTEUS, accompanied by LAUNCE, tries to encourage him. Launce, in soliloquy at the end, talks about his own love life.

(Launce has 23% of the lines; the remainder are evenly divided.)

WINTERS TALE	**2M,1W [1M,2W]**	**4:09**

Act V, sc. i, lines 1-83 (verse)

CLEOMENES/DION urges LEONTES to remarry for the good of the state. PAULINA reminds him he killed his first wife and makes him swear he will only marry when she selects the wife.

(Paulina has 46% of the lines, Leontes 29%. Cleomenes & Dion roles combined to one character, which could be played by woman.)

SCENES FOR FOUR AND FIVE ACTORS

Listed in alphabetical order by play titles, then in
Act/scene order.

ALL'S WELL	4W	5:09

Act III, sc. v, lines 1-104 (verse)

HELENA meets three Florentine women: the WIDOW,
DIANA, and MARIANA. She seeks lodging and they discuss Bertram and Parolles.

(Cut Parolles' line 91.)

ANTONY & CLEO.	4M	12:30

Act II, sc. ii, lines 1-250 (verse)

CAESAR and ANTONY patch up their quarrels by decid-
ing to have Antony marry Octavia. ENOBARUS describes
Cleopatra: "The barge she sat in..." Lepidus, Mecaenas, and
AGRIPPA participate.

*(Caesar has 19% of the lines, Antony has 30%. Incorporate
Lepidus and Mecaenas into the role of Agrippa and change names
and pronouns where necessary.)*

AS YOU LIKE IT	2M, 2W	6:15

Act I, sc. ii, lines 33-157 (prose)

CELIA and ROSALIND trade quips with TOUCHSTONE
and then find out about a wrestling match through a fop, LE
BEAU.

(Rosalind has 19% of the lines; Celia has 34%.)

CORIOLANUS	5M [4M, 1W; 3M, 2W]	12:12

Act IV, sc. v, lines 1-251 (prose/verse)

CORIOLANUS, banished from Rome, goes to his old
enemy, AUFIDIUS, and offers to betray Rome to the Volsces.
THREE SERVINGMEN discuss the implications of this.
Coriolanus and Aufidius, in verse, dominate the first half of
the scene; the Servants, in prose, the second. There is a cor-
responding shift from heroics to comedy.

(One or two of the Servants could be played by women.)

HAMLET	2M, 2W	11:18

Act IV, sc. v, lines 4-95, 115-219 and Act IV, sc. vii, lines 163-195 (verse/prose)

OPHELIA'S mad scene coupled with GERTRUDE'S report of her death to CLAUDIUS and LAERTES. The second scene is added to augment Gertrude's role. Ophelia must sing.

(Ophelia has 33% of the lines, Gertrude 19%. Gertrude begins by taking the Gentleman's lines 4 & following, continues with Horatio's lines 14-15, and then with her own lines.)

HENRY IV, Part II	2M, 2W	6:42

Act II, sc. iv, lines 119-252 (prose)

DOLL TEARSHEET and PISTOL begin a brawl when Doll rebuffs his attentions. MISTRESS QUICKLY restrains Pistol while FALSTAFF restrains Doll. Falstaff finally bullies Pistol outside by drawing his sword. A raucous, bawdy scene.

(Mistress Quickly and Falstaff each have 19% of the lines; Doll Tearsheet has 34%. Incorporate Bardolph into Mistress Quickly's part; replace references to Bardolph with Quickly's name. Falstaff takes the Pages lines; cut "sir" from line 245.)

HENRY V	3M, 1W	9:51

Act II, sc. i, lines 1-134 and Act II, sc. iii, lines 1-67 (prose)

MISTRESS QUICKLY has married PISTOL, and NYM, her rejected suitor, quarrels with Pistol and draws on him. BARDOLPH mediates. Mistress Quickly describes the death of Falstaff.

(In the first scene Bardolph finds an exit sometime between lines 68 and 85 and takes the rest of the speech and Bardolph's line 90. In the second scene, Nym takes the Boy's lines 42-44; Bardolph takes all the rest of the Boy's lines.)

HENRY VI, Part III	4M	5:30

Act II, sc. vi, lines 1-110 (verse)

Combine CLIFFORD'S soliloquy at his death with the scene for WARWICK, RICHARD and EDWARD, previously cited, where they find Clifford's corpse on the battlefield and know they have beaten Queen Margaret. Edward makes

Richard the Duke of Gloucester and Warwick sets off to France to bring Edward back a wife and queen.
(Not actually a four actor scene, but a soliloquy for one actor followed by a scene for three).

HENRY VIII 3M, 1W 10:42

Act I, sc. ii, lines 1-214 (verse)

QUEEN KATHARINE appeals to KING HENRY on behalf of the clothiers against a high tax Wolsey has levied against them in the king's name. WOLSEY produces a servant of Buckingham's, his SURVEYOR, to testify against Buckingham on a charge of treason. Henry believes him.
(Wolsey has less than 20% of the lines. Queen Katharine takes Norfolk's speech. Wolsey refers to the Surveyor when he is supposed to refer to his secretary.)

HENRY VIII 5M 9:09

Act V, sc. iii, lines 1-183 (verse)

The LORD CHANCELLOR, GARDINER, and CROMWELL call CRANMER to a council meeting where they accuse him of heresy. In desperation, Cranmer reveals a ring Henry VIII gave to him. HENRY then appears and declares Cranmer his new-born daughter's godfather.
(Incorporate the Lord Chamberlain's and Norfolk's lines into the Lord Chancellor's role. Incorporate the Keeper's, Surrey's, and Suffolk's lines into Cromwell's role. The Lord Chancellor has 10% of the lines; King Henry has nearly 30%.)

KING JOHN 3M, 1W 6:46

Act I, sc. i, lines 44-46, 49-181 (verse)

PHILIP THE BASTARD and his younger half-brother, ROBERT, come to JOHN and ELINOR for arbitration in their quarrel over their father's estate. Robert gets the land, the Bastard is knighted, and enters Elinor's service.
(Elinor takes Essex' lines 44-46, changing "liege" to "son." Elinor has 14% of the lines; the Bastard has 47%.)

KING JOHN 4M 7:27

Act IV, sc. iii, lines 11-159 (verse)

PHILIP THE BASTARD, PEMBROKE, and SALISBURY find Arthur's corpse. The Bastard prevents Pembroke and

Salisbury from killing Arthur's supposed murderer,
HUBERT. Pembroke and Salisbury defect to France while
Hubert and the Bastard go to the aid of King John.
*(Pembroke has 14% of the lines; the Bastard has 36%. Pembroke
takes Bigot's lines. Change "Lord Bigot" to "Lord Pembroke" in
line 103. Change pronouns as necessary.)*

KING JOHN   4M [3M, 1W]   5:54
Act V, sc. vii, lines 1-118 (verse)
    KING JOHN dies with PRINCE HENRY, PHILIP THE
BASTARD, and SALISBURY in attendance. Salisbury tells
the Bastard that the French are willing to negotiate a peace.
*(Incorporate all of Pembroke's lines into Salisbury's part. King
John must be carried on stage by extras or Prince Henry and Salis-
bury/Pembroke may simply walk to the actor who is across the
playing area from them. Prince Henry could be played by a
woman.)*

KING LEAR   4M [3M, 1W]   8:48 (or longer)
Act III, sc. ii, lines 39-96 and sc. iv, lines 1-119 (prose/verse)
    LEAR, the FOOL, and KENT meet and then come upon
EDGAR disguised as "Tom o' Bedlam" during a storm on
the heath. Notable for its dramatization of three varieties of
madness.
*(Kent has 16% of the lines; Lear has 42%. These two scenes easily
become one smooth scene if Lear and Kent don't exit but, instead,
come upon the hovel. The scene can be expanded in two ways: start
the first scene at line 1 for about 10:45 total length; add Act III, sc.
vi, lines 6-92 for about 15:05 total. The Fool could be played by a
woman.)*

LOVE'S LABOURS   4M   18:12
Act IV, sc. iii, lines 1-387 (verse)
    The KING, BIRON (Berowne), LONGAVILLE, and
DUMAIN: each enters and professes in turn his having
broken the common vow by falling in love. Each is over-
heard by those who have preceded him. Finally, Biron finds
an excuse for the vow-breaking.
*Longaville has 9% of the lines; Biron has 62%. many of Biron's
lines could be reassigned to others, or cut for a shorter scene. Much*

of the scene is in rhyme and in a variety of meters. Cut lines 188-205 and 210-214.)

MACBETH 1M, 3W 6:42

Act IV, sc. i, lines 1-134 (verse)

MACBETH and the THREE WITCHES. The scene requires three apparitions and Hecate also, but it could be done with the witches playing these parts, perhaps chorally. The witches dance.

(Macbeth has 40% of the lines.)

MEASURE 4M 12:09

Act II, sc. i, lines 41-289 (prose)

ELBOW brings POMPEY and FROTH before ESCALUS for trial for being bawds. A mildly comic scene.

(Froth has only 11 lines but he is essential to the scene. Incorporate Angelo's lines into Escalus' part. Cut "Go to; what quality are they of" from line 59 and also cut lines 139-143.)

MIDSUMMER 3M, 1W 5:18

Act I, sc. i, lines 20-127 (verse)

EGEUS demands of THESEUS that HERMIA (Egeus's daughter) be forced to marry LYSANDER and not Demetrius, who is her choice.

(Demetrius has two lines, 91-92, which must be cut. A little rewriting may be necessary because of his excision from the scene.)

MIDSUMMER 2M, 2W 11:09

Act III, sc. ii, lines 122-344 (verse)

Because of a misapplied love potion, HELENA, who had no lovers, now has two: LYSANDER and DEMETRIUS. HERMIA, who had two lovers, now has none. The women quarrel; the men go off to duel.

(Demetrius has 13% of the lines; Helena has 49%.)

MUCH ADO 4M 10:05

Act II, sc. iii, lines 7-44, 92-255 (prose)

DON PEDRO, CLAUDIO, and LEONATO trick the hiding BENEDICK into believing that Beatrice is dying of love for him.

(Claudio has 18% of the lines; Benedick has 31%. Benedick's part is largely a beginning and a closing soliloquy and reaction to the conversation of the other three. Begin with "I do much wonder..." in line 7.

OTHELLO	2M, 2W	8:33

Act IV, sc. ii, lines 1-171 (verse)

OTHELLO accuses DESDEMONA of being a whore; EMILIA is accused of being her bawd. IAGO pretends to sympathize with the women.

(Iago has only 14 lines—8%—but the part could be augmented by introducing the scene with a speech by Iago—perhaps Act II, sc. iii, lines 342-368.)

PERICLES	4M	8:36

Act II, sc. i, lines 1-172 (prose/verse)

PERICLES, cast up after a shipwreck, meets THREE FISHERMEN who discuss the world in metaphors. Pericles speaks verse; the others speak prose.

The 3rd Fisherman has 10% of the lines; Pericles has 45%. The balance could be improved by some re-distribution of the fisherman's lines.)

PERICLES	2M, 2W	8:05

Act IV, sc. ii, lines 1-163 (prose)

PANDAR, BAWD, and BOULT buy MARINA from pirates and instruct her in her duties as a whore. The presence of the pirates should be suggested.

(The balance is not too good: Marina has 11% of the lines; Bawd has 47%. Cut the Pirate's line 46.)

PERICLES	2M, 2W	10:36

Act IV, sc. vi, lines 1-212 (prose/verse)

MARINA, captive in a brothel, is offered to LYSIMACHUS by BAWD and BOULT. She converts him to continence, he gives her money, and she buys her way out.

(Bawd takes Pandar's lines 1-2 and 14-15.)

RICHARD II	3M, 1W [2M, 2W]	9:00

Act V, sc. ii, lines 46-84, 111-117 and sc. iii, lines 1-12, 23-146 (verse)

The DUKE OF YORK and his DUCHESS discover that their son, AUMERLE, is involved in a treasonous plot against BOLINGBROOKE (Henry IV). Aumerle rushes to the King to beg for mercy, York follows demanding punishment, and the Duchess follows and convinces the King to pardon Aumerle. "Our scene is altered from a serious thing,/And now changed to 'The Beggar and the King.'"
(Aumerle has 15% of the lines; the Duchess has 35%. The larger roles could easily be cut, if desired, to make Aumerle a relatively larger part. Aumerle, a very young man, could be played by a woman.)

RICHARD III	**2M, 2W**	**13:45**

Act I, sc. iii, lines 1-16, 42-279, 299-319 (verse)

GLOUCESTER (later RICHARD III) quarrels with QUEEN ELIZABETH and RIVERS. QUEEN MARGARET, like a fury, points out their guilt in the sorrows of the House of Lancaster.
(Rivers has 12% of the lines, Margaret 40%. Cut the first half of Rivers' line 305. Rivers takes all the other lords' lines)

RICHARD III	**4M [3M, 1W; 2M, 2W]**	**4:51**

Act III, sc. i, lines 61-157 (verse)

The young DUKE OF YORK and his brother, PRINCE EDWARD, make GLOUCESTER (later RICHARD III) look like a fool with their quick wit. BUCKINGHAM, who is plotting the boys' deaths with Gloucester, plays along with the boys. The Prince and the Duke are young boys.
(The balance is poor: Buckingham has 13% of the lines; Gloucester and Prince Edward each have 32%. Some reassignment of lines among the characters could improve this. Prince Edward and/or the Duke of York could be played by a woman.)

RICHARD III	**1M, 3W**	**9:45**

Act IV, sc. iv, lines 1-195 (verse)

QUEEN MARGARET, QUEEN ELIZABETH, and the DUCHESS OF YORK keen over the blood and sorrow KING RICHARD has dealt them: the "weeping queens" scene.
(King Richard has 10% of the lines; Queen Margaret has 50%.)

ROMEO & JULIET	**4M**	**7:06**

Act III, sc. i, lines 1-142 (prose/verse)

MERCUTIO and BENVOLIO meet TYBALT. Mercutio and Tybalt fight. ROMEO interferes, Mercutio is killed, and Romeo kills Tybalt. All but Benvolio must be good fencers. (*Tybalt has 10% of the lines; Mercutio has 48%.*)

ROMEO & JULIET	**1M, 3W**	**9:09**

Act III, sc. v, lines 60-242 (verse)

CAPULET and LADY CAPULET tell JULIET she must marry Paris on Thursday. Juliet refuses. Because the NURSE also insists on this marriage, Juliet determines to seek favorable advice from Friar Laurence or die. (*The Nurse has 10% of the lines; Juliet has almost 40%.*)

TAMING of the SHREW	**4M [3M, 1W; 2M, 2W]**	**7:18**

Induction, sc. ii, lines 1-146 (verse)

SLY is convinced by a LORD and a SERVANT that he is himself a lord, and that the PAGE is his wife. (*The three Servants are played by one actor. The Page takes the Messenger's lines. The Page has 16% of the lines; Sly has 37%. The Page was written as a man dressed as a woman; obviously the role could easily be played by a woman, as could the Servant.*)

TEMPEST	**3M, 1W [2M, 2W]**	**6:21 *or* 7:06**

Act I, sc. ii, lines (1-15 and) 375-501 (verse)

PROSPERO, with ARIEL'S help, brings FERDINAND and MIRANDA together to cause them to fall in love. Then, Prospero pretends to set difficulties in their way. Ariel's role is virtually all singing. (*Ariel has 16% of the lines and Miranda 17%; to expand Miranda's role to about 25% and the scene to 7:06, add lines 1-15 of the scene. Ariel could be played by a woman.*)

TITUS ANDRONICUS	**3M, 1W [2M, 2W]**	**6:27**

Act IV, sc. i, lines 1-129 (verse)

The mutilated, mute, LAVINIA communicates to TITUS, MARCUS, and YOUNG LUCIUS the names of her ravishers by writing with a stick held between her stumps. Lavinia has no lines--mime only.

(Lucius has 19% of the lines, Titus 45%. Young Lucius could be played by a woman.)

TROILUS & CRESSIDA 4M 19:36
Act I, sc. iii, lines 1-392 (verse)

AGAMEMNON, ULYSSES, and NESTOR discuss Achilles' absence as the reason why the Greeks cannot destroy Troy. AENEAS brings them a challenge from Hector to single combat. Ulysses and Nestor find in this a plan to reinvolve Achilles.

(Aeneas has 15% of the lines, Ulysses has 45%. Ulysses' part can be trimmed to create a shorter, better balanced scene. Cut the reference to Menelaus in l. 213 and assign Menelaus' l. 114 to Nestor.)

TWELFTH NIGHT 4M, 1W [3M,2W] 21:48
Act II, sc. iii, lines 1-208 and Act II, sc. v, lines 1-228 (prose)

MALVOLIO reprimands SIR TOBY, SIR ANDREW, the CLOWN (FESTE), and MARIA for drinking and carousing. They avenge themselves on him by writing a letter, purportedly by Olivia, making Malvolio think Olivia is in love with him. They hide and watch him make a fool of himself when he finds the letter.

(Maria has 14% of the lines; Malvolio has 30%. Feste takes Fabian's lines in the second scene. Feste/Fabian could be played by a woman.)

TWO GENTLEMEN 2M, 2W [1M, 3W] 5:36
Act IV, sc. ii, lines 27-141 (prose/verse)

The HOST brings JULIA to where she may hear PROTEUS, whom she loves, serenading SILVIA, whom he loves. Proteus must sing; he performs "Who is Sylvia? what is she?"

(The Host could be played by a woman. Cut lines 82-84.)

TWO GENTLEMEN 2M, 2W 5:06
Act V, sc. iv, lines 19-120 (verse)

PROTEUS and JULIA, VALENTINE and SILVIA are reconciled to each other and pair off properly after the exposure of Proteus' infidelity and Julia's disguise.

(Proteus has 38% of the lines.)

TWO NOBLE KINSMEN   3M, 1W [2M, 2W; 1M, 3W]   15:30

Act IV, sc. i, lines 32-151; Act IV, sc. iii, lines 1-81; and Act V, sc. ii, lines 1-99, 105-113 (prose/verse)

Three scenes involving the care and cure of the JAILER'S DAUGHTER by the DOCTOR assisted by the JAILER and the WOOER. An imitation (by Fletcher) of the Ophelia mad scenes: pathos and sexual imagery.

(The Jailer has 15% of the lines; the Daughter has 36%. The Jailer takes the lines of the two friends in Act IV, sc. i; the Doctor plays the Brother in Act IV, sc. iii. The Jailer and/or the Doctor could be women.)

WINTER'S TALE   3M, 1W   19:12

Act I, sc. ii, lines 1-465 (verse)

Virtually the whole first act. HERMIONE urges POLIXENES to extend his visit. Her friendliness to him makes her husband, LEONTES, jealous, and he orders CAMILLO to kill him. But Camillo warns Polixenes and helps him escape.

(Hermione has 15% of the lines. Cut the role of Mamilius. Cut from line 119, "Mamilius...", to line 146, "...of my brows.", line 151, "How sometimes..." to line 177, "...my heart", line 187, "Go, play..." to line 208, "...some comfort", and cut line 211, "Go play...".)

Notes:

INDEX: Women's Monologues, by Time

(✗ indicates a "chestnut," an overdone piece.)

CORDELIA .... *King Lear* 0:51 3
QUEEN MARGARET ..... *Henry VI, Part III* 0:51 13
QUEEN MARGARET ..... *Richard III* 0:54 14
VIOLA .... *Twelfth Night* 0:58 16
LADY MACBETH .... *Macbeth* ....1:00 ✗ 8
MISTRESS QUICKLY ..... *Henry V* ....1:00 ✗ 9
PHEBE .... *As You Like It* 1:00 10
QUEEN ELIZABETH .... *Richard III* 1:00 11
MISTRESS QUICKLY ..... *Henry IV, Part II* 1:03 9
CLEOPATRA .... *Antony & Cleopatra* 1:06 1
PORTIA .... *Merchant of Venice* ....1:06 ✗ ... 11
QUEEN KATHARINE .... *Henry VIII* 1:06 11
CLEOPATRA .... *Antony & Cleopatra* 1:09 1
PORTIA .... *Julius Caesar* 1:09 10
PORTIA .... *Merchant of Venice* 1:09 10
PORTIA .... *Merchant of Venice* 1:12 10
ROSALIND .... *As You Like It* 1:12 15
QUEEN .... *Richard II* 1:13 11
VIOLA .... *Twelfth Night* ....1:15 ✗ ... 16
DUCHESS OF YORK ...... *Richard III* 1:18 3
HELENA .... *Midsummer* 1:18 4
JAILER'S DAUGHTER .... *Two Noble Kinsmen* 1:18 6
JULIA .... *Two Gentlemen* ....1:18 ✗ 7
MISTRESS QUICKLY ..... *Henry IV, Part II* 1:18 8
DUCHESS OF YORK ...... *Richard III* 1:21 3
HELENA .... *All's Well* 1:21 4
IMOGEN .... *Cymbeline* 1:21 5
JULIA .... *Two Gentlemen* 1:21 7
QUEEN MARGARET ..... *Henry VI, Part III* 1:21 13
QUEEN MARGARET ..... *Richard III* 1:21 14
ANNE .... *Richard III* 1:24 1
EMILIA .... *2 Noble Kinsmen* 1:24 4
LUCIANA .... *Comedy of Errors* 1:24 8
[PUCK] .... *Midsummer* 1:26 18
JOAN LA PUCELLE ...... *Henry VI, Part I* 1:27 6
LADY PERCY .... *Henry IV, Part I* 1:27 8
ROSALIND .... *As You Like It* ....1:27 ✗ ... 15
[BOY] .... *Henry V* 1:27 17
CLEOPATRA .... *Antony & Cleopatra* 1:30 1
ANNE .... *Richard III* 1:36 1
EMILIA .... *Othello* 1:36 3
JAILER'S DAUGHTER .... *Two Noble Kinsmen* 1:36 6
[PROLOGUE] .... *Henry VIII* 1:36 18
JAILER'S DAUGHTER .... *Two Noble Kinsmen* 1:39 5
JULIET .... *Romeo & Juliet* ....1:39 ✗ 7
CLEOPATRA .... *Antony & Cleopatra* ....1:41 ✗ 2

JOAN LA PUCELLE ...... *Henry VI, Part I* 1:42 6
[CHORUS] .... *Henry V* .... 1:42 ✘ ... 17
QUEEN MARGARET ..... *Henry VI, Part II* 1:45 13
[CHORUS] .... *Henry V* 1:45 17
ROSALIND .... *As You Like It* 1:48 15
[PIRITHOUS] .... *Two Noble Kinsmen* 1:48 18
ADRIANA .... *Comedy of Errors* 1:51 1
EMILIA .... *Two Noble Kinsmen* 1:51 4
LADY PERCY .... *Henry IV, Part II* 1:51 8
TITANIA .... *Midsummer* 1:51 16
[EPILOGUE] .... *Henry IV, Part II* 1:51 17
DUCHESS of GLOU. ...... *Henry VI, Part II* 1:54 3
JAILER'S DAUGHTER .... *Two Noble Kinsmen* 1:54 6
PHEBE .... *As You Like It* 1:54 10
QUEEN MARGARET ..... *Henry VI, Part II* 1:54 12
QUEEN MARGARET ..... *Henry VI, Part III* 1:54 13
JAILER'S DAUGHTER .... *Two Noble Kinsmen* 1:57 5
QUEEN MARGARET ..... *Henry VI, Part II* 2:00 12
QUEEN MARGARET ..... *Richard III* 2:00 14
[RUMOUR] .... *Henry IV, Part II* 2:00 18
QUEEN MARGARET ..... *Richard III* 2:03 14
IMOGEN .... *Cymbeline* 2:06 5
[CHORUS] .... *Henry V* 2:06 17
QUEEN MARGARET ..... *Henry VI, Part III* 2:09 13
CONSTANCE .... *King John* 2:12 2
KATHARINA .... *Taming of the Shrew* ...... 2:12 ✘ 7
QUEEN KATHARINE .... *Henry VIII* 2:12 12
JULIET .... *Romeo & Juliet* .... 2:15 ✘ 7
NURSE .... *Romeo & Juliet* .... 2:15 ✘ 9
QUEEN KATHARINE .... *Henry VIII* 2:15 11
[CHORUS] .... *Henry V* 2:15 17
PORTIA .... *Merchant of Venice* 2:21 11
LADY MACBETH .... *Macbeth* .... 2:23 ✘ 4
ROSALIND .... *As You Like It* 2:24 15
PAULINA .... *Winter's Tale* 2:39 9
[CHORUS] .... *Henry V* .... 2:39 ... 17
ROSALIND .... *As You Like It* 2:48 15
VOLUMNIA .... *Coriolanus* 2:49 16
PORTIA .... *Julius Caesar* .... 2:51 ✘ ... 10
QUEEN MARGARET ..... *Richard III* 2:51 14
JULIET .... *Romeo & Juliet* 2:55 7
[FIRST PLAYER] .... *Hamlet* 2:56 18
DUCHESS of GLOU. ...... *Richard II* 2:57 3
EMILIA .... *Two Noble Kinsmen* 3:00 4
MISTRESS QUICKLY ..... *Merry Wives of Windsor* ... 3:12 9
CONSTANCE .... *King John* 3:14 2
QUEEN MARGARET ..... *Henry VI, Part II* 3:15 13
HELENA .... *Midsummer* 3:21 4
CONSTANCE .... *King John* 3:31 2

OPHELIA .... *Hamlet* 3:45 9
QUEEN KATHARINE .... *Henry VIII* 3:47 11
QUEEN KATHARINE .... *Henry VIII* 3:49 11
HERMIONE .... *Winter's Tale* 3:53 5
QUEEN MARGARET ..... *Richard III* 4:03 15
VOLUMNIA .... *Coriolanus* 4:23 16
IMOGEN .... *Cymbeline* 4:26 5
CONSTANCE .... *King John* 6:45 2
JAILER'S DAUGHTER .... *Two Noble Kinsmen* 6:48 6

INDEX: Men's Monologues, by Time

Character	Play	Time	pg#
(✗ indicates a "chestnut," an overdone piece.)			
DOGBERRY	*Much Ado*	0:45 ✗	30
FALSTAFF	*Henry IV, Part I*	0:48 ✗	32
PROSPERO	*The Tempest*	0:48 ✗	53
CADE	*Henry VI, Part II*	0:51	25
WOLSEY	*Henry VIII*	0:51	61
ARMADO	*Love's Labours Lost*	1:03	21
CAESAR	*Julius Caesar*	1:03 ✗	26
EDGAR	*King Lear*	1:03	30
FALSTAFF	*Henry IV, Part I*	1:03 ✗	32
MESSENGER	*Henry VI, Part III*	1:03	48
RICHARD III	*Richard III*	1:03	57
ANTONY	*Julius Caesar*	1:06 ✗	20
BRUTUS	*Julius Caesar*	1:06	23
CLARENCE	*Henry VI, Part III*	1:06	28
EDMUND	*King Lear*	1:06 ✗	30
OTHELLO	*Othello*	1:06 ✗	50
RICHARD	*Richard II*	1:06	55
WOLSEY	*Henry VIII*	1:06	61
LEAR	*King Lear*	1:07	45
AARON	*Titus Andronicus*	1:09	19
CONSTABLE of FRANCE	*Henry V*	1:09	29
DUKE SENIOR	*As You Like It*	1:09	30
FALSTAFF	*Henry IV, Part I*	1:09	31
HENRY IV	*Henry IV, Part II*	1:09	39
LEAR	*King Lear*	1:09 ✗	45
PORTER	*Macbeth*	1:09 ✗	51
PORTER'S MAN	*Henry VIII*	1:09	51
PRINCE HAL	*Henry IV, Part I*	1:09	52
RICHARD III	*Richard III*	1:09	56
TYRREL	*Richard III*	1:09	60
WOLSEY	*Henry VIII*	1:09	61
ANTIPHOLUS of SYR.	*Comedy of Errors*	1:12	20
ANTONY	*Antony & Cleopatra*	1:12	20
HAMLET	*Hamlet*	1:12 ✗	37
LEONATO	*Much Ado*	1:12	46
MARULLUS	*Julius Caesar*	1:12	47
WARWICK	*Henry VI, Part III*	1:12	61
CADE	*Henry VI, Part II*	1:15	25
FALSTAFF	*Henry IV, Part I*	1:15	31
HASTINGS	*Richard III*	1:15	37
HENRY IV	*Henry IV, Part II*	1:15	38
MACBETH	*Macbeth*	1:15	47
WOLSEY	*Henry VIII*	1:15	61
ANGELO	*Measure for Measure*	1:16	19

CADE . . . . *Henry VI, Part II* 1:18 25
EXETER . . . . *Henry V* 1:18 31
JACQUES . . . . *As You Like It* . . . . 1:18 ✗ . . . 44
PRINCE HAL . . . . *Henry IV, Part II* 1:18 53
RICHARD III . . . . *Richard III* 1:18 56
YORK . . . . *Henry VI, Part III* 1:18 62
IAGO . . . . *Othello* 1:20 44
PETRUCHIO . . . . *Taming of the Shrew* 1:20 51
BRUTUS . . . . *Julius Caesar* 1:21 23
BUCKINGHAM . . . . *Richard III* 1:21 25
FALSTAFF . . . . *Henry IV, Part II* 1:21 32
IAGO . . . . *Othello* 1:21 44
POSTHUMUS . . . . *Cymbeline* 1:21 52
AENEAS . . . . *Troilus & Cressida* 1:22 19
CAESAR . . . . *Antony & Cleopatra* 1:23 25
BENEDICK . . . . *Much Ado* 1:24 22
CLOTEN . . . . *Cymbeline* 1:24 29
FLAVIUS . . . . *Timon of Athens* 1:24 33
MACBETH . . . . *Macbeth* . . . . 1:24 ✗ . . . 46
PRINCE HAL . . . . *Henry IV, Part II* 1:24 52
SHYLOCK . . . . *Merchant of Venice* 1:24 58
TOUCHSTONE . . . . *As You Like It* 1:24 60
PUCK . . . . *Midsummer* 1:26 54
BOY . . . . *Henry V* 1:27 23
CASCA . . . . *Julius Caesar* 1:27 26
CRANMER . . . . *Henry VIII* 1:27 29
DON JOHN . . . . *Much Ado* 1:27 30
FORD . . . . *Merry Wives* 1:27 33
GLOUCESTER . . . . *Henry VI, Part II* 1:27 35
TIMON . . . . *Timon of Athens* 1:27 59
AGAMEMNON . . . . *Troilus & Cressida* 1:28 19
BOLINGBROOKE . . . . *Richard II* 1:30 23
CAESAR . . . . *Julius Caesar* 1:30 26
CLIFFORD . . . . *Henry VI, Part III* 1:30 29
FR. LAURENCE . . . . *Romeo & Juliet* . . . . 1:30 ✗ . . . 33
GLOUCESTER . . . . *Henry VI, Part II* 1:30 35
HAMLET . . . . *Hamlet* . . . . 1:30 ✗ . . . 36
HENRY IV . . . . *Henry IV, Part II* 1:30 38
HOTSPUR . . . . *Henry IV, Part I* 1:30 42
MACBETH . . . . *Macbeth* . . . . 1:30 ✗ . . . 47
RICHARD III . . . . *Richard III* . . . . 1:30 ✗ . . . 57
AUFIDIUS . . . . *Coriolanus* 1:33 21
BIRON (Berowne) . . . . *Love's Labours Lost* 1:33 23
HENRY IV . . . . *Henry IV, Part II* 1:33 38
PRINCE HAL . . . . *Henry IV, Part I* 1:33 52
SHYLOCK . . . . *Merchant of Venice* . . . . 1:33 ✗ . . . 58
BENEDICK . . . . *Much Ado* 1:36 22
CASCA . . . . *Julius Caesar* 1:36 26
EDWARD . . . . *Richard III* 1:36 31

LEAR .... *King Lear* 1:36 45
OLD TALBOT .... *Henry VI, Part I* 1:36 49
PROLOGUE .... *Henry VIII* 1:36 53
WARWICK .... *Henry IV, Part II* 1:36 61
GENTLEMAN .... *Henry VIII* 1:39 34
GLOUCESTER .... *Henry VI, Part III* 1:39 35
HAMLET .... *Hamlet* .... 1:39 ✗ ... 36
HENRY IV .... *Henry IV, Part I* 1:39 38
LAUNCELOT .... *Merchant of Venice* .... 1:39 ✗ ... 45
POSTHUMUS .... *Cymbeline* 1:39 51
RICHARD III .... *Richard III* 1:39 56
HAMLET .... *Hamlet* 1:40 36
GOWER .... *Pericles* 1:41 35
CAPTAIN .... *Henry VI, Part II* 1:42 26
CHORUS .... *Henry V* .... 1:42 ✗ ... 27
CLIFFORD .... *Henry VI, Part III* 1:42 28
FRIAR FRANCIS .... *Much Ado* 1:42 34
HENRY V .... *Henry V* .... 1:42 ✗ ... 40
MACBETH .... *Macbeth* .... 1:42 ✗ ... 47
PRINCE HAL .... *Henry IV, Part I* 1:42 52
ANTONY .... *Julius Caesar* .... 1:45 ✗ ... 20
ARCITE .... *Two Noble Kinsmen* 1:45 21
CHORUS .... *Henry V* 1:45 27
CLIFFORD .... *Henry VI, Part II* 1:45 28
CORIOLANUS .... *Coriolanus* 1:45 29
HAMLET .... *Hamlet* .... 1:45 ✗ ... 37
HENRY IV .... *Henry IV, Part II* 1:45 38
LAUNCE .... *Two Gentlemen* 1:45 44
LORENZO .... *Merchant of Venice* 1:45 46
POSTHUMUS .... *Cymbeline* 1:45 51
RICHARD .... *Richard II* 1:45 55
RICHMOND .... *Richard III* 1:45 57
CARLISLE .... *Richard II* 1:48 26
FALSTAFF .... *Henry IV, Part II* 1:48 32
HENRY V .... *Henry V* 1:48 40
PIRITHOUS .... *Two Noble Kinsmen* 1:48 51
TOUCHSTONE .... *As You Like It* 1:48 60
ORSINO .... *Twelfth Night* .... 1:49 ✗ ... 50
BOLINGBROOKE .... *Richard II* 1:51 23
CLAUDIO .... *Measure for Measure* 1:51 28
CORIOLANUS .... *Coriolanus* 1:51 29
EPILOGUE .... *Henry IV, Part II* 1:51 31
EXETER .... *Henry V* 1:51 31
LEONATO .... *Much Ado* 1:51 46
RICHARD III .... *Richard III* .... 1:51 ✗ ... 56
BASTARD .... *King John* 1:54 21
BUCKINGHAM .... *Richard III* 1:54 24
CLAUDIUS .... *Hamlet* .... 1:54 ✗ ... 28
GAUNT .... *Richard II* .... 1:54 ✗ ... 34

HENRY VI .... *Henry VI, Part III* ....1:54..... 41
HOTSPUR .... *Henry IV, Part I* ....1:54..... 42
MESSENGER .... *Henry VI, Part I* ....1:54..... 48
NORFOLK .... *Henry VIII* ....1:54..... 49
RICHARD III .... *Richard III* ....1:54..... 57
WARWICK .... *Henry VI, Part III* ....1:54..... 61
YORK .... *Richard II* ....1:54..... 63
BASTARD .... *King John* ....1:57..... 22
BENEDICK .... *Much Ado* ....1:57..... 22
LEWIS .... *King John* ....1:57..... 46
LORD .... *As You Like It* ....1:57..... 46
MELUN .... *King John* ....1:57..... 48
PRINCE HAL .... *Henry IV, Part II* ....1:57..... 53
HAMLET .... *Hamlet* ....2:00..... 37
OBERON .... *Midsummer* ....2:00..... 49
RUMOUR .... *Henry IV, Part II* ....2:00..... 58
TITUS .... *Titus Andronicus* ....2:00..... 59
YORK .... *Richard II* ....2:00..... 63
BASTARD .... *King John* ....2:03..... 21
FALSTAFF .... *Henry IV, Part I* ....2:03..... 32
HOTSPUR .... *Henry IV, Part I* ....2:03 ✘... 42
IACHIMO .... *Cymbeline* ....2:03..... 43
RICHARD III .... *Richard III* ....2:03 ✘... 56
TIMON .... *Timon of Athens* ....2:03..... 59
PROSPERO .... *The Tempest* ....2:04 ✘... 53
CHORUS .... *Henry V* ....2:06..... 27
HENRY V .... *Henry V* ....2:06..... 40
JOHN .... *King John* ....2:06..... 44
ANTIGONUS .... *Winter's Tale* ....2:09..... 19
ANTONY .... *Julius Caesar* ....2:09..... 20
BUCKINGHAM .... *Henry VIII* ....2:09..... 24
FALSTAFF .... *Henry IV, Part II* ....2:09..... 32
GARDENER .... *Richard II* ....2:09..... 34
HENRY IV .... *Henry IV, Part II* ....2:09..... 39
HENRY V .... *Henry V* ....2:09..... 40
PROTEUS .... *Two Gentlemen* ....2:09..... 54
TITUS .... *Titus Andronicus* ....2:09..... 59
HENRY VIII .... *Henry VIII* ....2:10..... 42
LAUNCE .... *Two Gentlemen* ....2:12..... 45
PANDULPH .... *King John* ....2:12..... 50
PRINCE HAL .... *Henry IV, Part II* ....2:12..... 53
SUFFOLK .... *Henry VI, Part II* ....2:12..... 59
HENRY VI .... *Henry VI, Part III* ....2:13..... 41
BASTARD .... *King John* ....2:15..... 22
BURGUNDY .... *Henry V* ;................2:15..... 25
CHORUS .... *Henry V* ....2:15..... 28
FALSTAFF .... *Henry IV, Part II* ....2:15..... 32
ULYSSES .... *Troilus & Cressida* ....2:17..... 60
AUFIDIUS .... *Coriolanus* ....2:18..... 21

COMINIUS	*Coriolanus*	2:18	29
ENOBARBUS	*Antony & Cleopatra*	2:18	31
HENRY IV	*Henry IV, Part II*	2:18	39
RICHARD III	*Richard III*	2:18	57
SHALLOW	*Henry IV, Part II*	2:18	58
YORK	*Henry VI, Part II*	2:18	62
BRUTUS	*Julius Caesar*	2:21	24
MARCUS	*Titus Andronicus*	2:21	47
OLIVER	*As You Like It*	2:21	49
ROMEO	*Romeo & Juliet*	2:21	57
TIMON	*Timon of Athens*	2:21	59
HENRY V	*Henry V*	2:24 ✘	40
POSTHUMUS	*Cymbeline*	2:24	52
RICHARD	*Richard II*	2:24	54
CRANMER	*Henry VIII*	2:27	30
JAQUES	*As You Like It*	2:27	44
HAMLET	*Hamlet*	2:30 ✘	36
MERCUTIO	*Romeo & Juliet*	2:30 ✘	48
RICHARD	*Richard II*	2:30	54
TIMON	*Timon of Athens*	2:30	59
FR. LAURENCE	*Romeo & Juliet*	2:33	34
FRANCE	*All's Well*	2:33	34
MENENIUS	*Coriolanus*	2:33	48
RICHARD III	*Richard III*	2:33	57
SUFFOLK	*Henry VI, Part II*	2:33	58
HENRY V	*Henry V*	2:36	39
YORK	*Richard II*	2:36	62
ADAM	*As You Like It*	2:39	19
CHORUS	*Henry V*	2:39	27
IACHIMO	*Cymbeline*	2:39	43
YORK	*Henry VI, Part II*	2:39	62
HENRY VI	*Henry VI, Part III*	2:42	41
JOHN	*King John*	2:42	44
IAGO	*Othello*	2:43	43
RICHARD	*Richard II*	2:48 ✘	54
YORK	*Henry VI, Part III*	2:48	62
RICHARD	*Richard II*	2:51	54
SHYLOCK	*Merchant of Venice*	2:51	58
BRUTUS	*Julius Caesar*	2:54	24
HENRY VIII	*Henry VIII*	2:54	42
FIRST PLAYER	*Hamlet*	2:56	33
HAMLET	*Hamlet*	2:57 ✘	36
HOTSPUR	*Henry IV, Part I*	3:00	42
BUCKINGHAM	*Richard III*	3:03	24
OTHELLO	*Othello*	3:03	50
FALSTAFF	*Merry Wives*	3:06	33
MOROCCO	*Merchant of Venice*	3:06	49
ULYSSES	*Troilus & Cressida*	3:06	60
WOLSEY	*Henry VIII*	3:06	62

ARAGON .... *Merchant of Venice* 3:08 20
CANTERBURY .... *Henry V* 3:09 26
PANDULPH .... *King John* 3:15 50
RICHARD .... *Richard II* 3:16 55
CLARENCE .... *Richard III* 3:17 28
HENRY IV .... *Henry IV, Part II* 3:18 38
PALAMON .... *Two Noble Kinsmen* 3:24 50
CASSIUS .... *Julius Caesar* 3:27 27
CASSIUS .... *Julius Caesar* 3:30 27
HENRY V .... *Henry V* 3:34 40
BUCKINGHAM .... *Henry VIII* 3:35 24
GLOUCESTER .... *Henry VI, Part III* 3:36 35
MENENIUS .... *Coriolanus* 3:39 48
POLONIUS .... *Hamlet* .... 3:46 ✗ ... 51
BIRON (Berowne) .... *Love's Labours Lost* 3:48 23
HENRY VIII .... *Henry VIII* 3:57 41
GHOST .... *Hamlet* 3:59 34
MORE .... *Sir Thomas More* 4:03 48
BELARIUS .... *Cymbeline* 4:21 22
IAGO .... *Othello* 4:21 43
HAMLET .... *Hamlet* 4:24 36
IAGO .... *Othello* 4:24 43
LEAR .... *King Lear* 4:24 45
HENRY V .... *Henry V* 4:42 39
RICHARD .... *Richard II* 5:15 55
HENRY IV .... *Henry IV, Part I* 5:48 38
MALVOLIO .... *Twelfth Night* .... 5:48 ✗ ... 47
RICHARD .... *Richard II* 5:54 55
HENRY V .... *Henry V* 5:57 41
ULYSSES .... *Troilus & Cressida* 6:33 60
HAMLET .... *Hamlet* 7:33 37
ANTONY .... *Julius Caesar* .... 8:00 ✗ ... 20

INDEX: Scenes, by Time

(✘ indicates a "chestnut," an overdone piece.)

Play	Characters	Time	pg#
MUCH ADO	Beatrice/Benedick	1:39	102
MACBETH	Macbeth/Macduff	1:42	76
RICHARD II	Queen/Gardener	2:00	103
TWELFTH NIGHT	Maria/Feste	2:00	106
HENRY IV, Part I	Prince Hal/Hotspur	2:03	71
MERCHANT of VENICE	Portia/Bassanio	2:03	100
AS YOU LIKE IT	Celia/Rosalind	2:06	89
HENRY IV, Part I	Mistress Quickly/Falstaff	2:06	95
TIMON of ATHENS	Sempronius/Servant	2:06	82
HENRY VI, Part III	Clifford/Rutland	2:09	73
AS YOU LIKE IT	Jaques/Orlando	2:12	66
KING JOHN	Hubert/Philip	2:12	75
MIDSUMMER	Hermia/Demetrius	2:15	101
TROILUS & CRESSIDA	Pandarus/[Servant]	2:15	83, 106
HAMLET	Ophelia/Polonius	2:17	95
TWELFTH NIGHT	Maria/Sir Toby Belch	2:18	106
KING LEAR	Lear/[Foo]l	2:21	75, 98
HENRY VI, Part II	Duchess/Hume	2:24	96
AS YOU LIKE IT	Celia/Rosalind	2:27	89
CORIOLANUS	Cominius/Menenius	2:27	67
JULIUS CAESAR	Calpurnia/Caesar	2:27	97
ROMEO & JULIET	Gregory/Sampson	2:30	80
WINTER'S TALE	Archidamus/Camillo	2:30	86
WINTER'S TALE	[Archidamus]/[Camillo]	2:30	92, 108
PERICLES	Dionyzia/Cleon	2:33	103
KING LEAR	Cordelia/Lear	2:35	98
MIDSUMMER	Hermia/Lysander	2:36	101
TWO NOBLE KINSMEN	Arcite/Palamon	2:39	85
KING LEAR	Edmund/Gloucester	2:40	76
MERCHANT of VENICE	Salanio/Salarino	2:40	77
HAMLET	Hamlet/Claudius	2:42	69
TITUS ANDRONICUS	Tamora/Aaron	2:42	105
HENRY VI, Part II	Duch./Duke of Glou.	2:43	96
WINTER'S TALE	Perdita/Florizel	2:43	108
HENRY IV, Part I	Gadshill/Chamberlain	2:45	70
MUCH ADO	Beatrice/Benedick	2:45	102
MIDSUMMER	Puck/Fairy	2:47	78
MIDSUMMER	[Puck]/[Fairy]	2:47	91, 101
HENRY V	Henry/Montjoy	2:48	72
TEMPEST	Prospero/Caliban	2:48	81
MERCHANT of VENICE	Jessica/Lorenzo	2:50	100
MIDSUMMER	Helena/Demetrius	2:51	101
RICHARD II	Bolingbrooke/Gaunt	2:51	79
MIDSUMMER	Helena/Lysander	2:52	101
CYMBELINE	Imogen/Cloten	2:54	94

AS YOU LIKE IT .... Celia/Rosalind 2:57 89
MERCHANT of VENICE .. Portia/Bassanio...........2:57 100
ANTONY & CLEOPATRA . Cleopatra/Antony 2:59 93
CORIOLANUS .... Adrian/Nicanor 2:85 67
KING LEAR .... Regan/Lear 3:00 98
ROMEO & JULIET .... Nurse/Romeo 3:00 104
TWELFTH NIGHT .... Viola/Captain 3:00 106
HENRY VI, Part I .... Joan/Warwick(York) 3:01 96
ANTONY & CLEOPATRA . Enobarbus/Menas 3:03 65
TIMON of ATHENS ...... Flaminius/Lucullus 3:03 82
HENRY IV, Part I .... Prince Hal/Poins 3:06 70
TWO GENTLEMEN ...... Launce/Speed 3:06 84
TWO GENTLEMEN ...... [Launce]/[Speed] ....3:06 . 92, 107
ROMEO & JULIET .... Juliet/Romeo 3:08 104
HENRY V .... Katharine/Alice 3:12 90
OTHELLO .... Desdemona/Othello 3:12 102
ROMEO & JULIET .... Romeo/Fr. Laurence 3:12 81
KING JOHN .... Salisbury/Lewis 3:13 75
AS YOU LIKE IT .... Jaques/Amiens 3:15 65
RICHARD II .... Richard/Scroop...........3:15 80
MERCHANT of VENICE .. Portia/Bassanio...........3:17 100
CORIOLANUS .... Brutus/Sicinius 3:18 66
HENRY VI, Part III .... Lady Grey/Edward 3:18 97
OTHELLO .... Desdemona/Othello 3:19 102
HENRY VIII .... 3M 3:21 114
TWELFTH NIGHT .... Andrew/Toby 3:21 83
HENRY VIII .... Porter/Porter's Man 3:24 74
HENRY VIII .... Henry/Wolsey 3:25 74
ROMEO & JULIET .... 3M [2M, 1W] 3:27 118
TWO GENTLEMEN ...... Proteus/Valentine 3:27 84
ROMEO & JULIET .... Romeo/Mercutio 3:29 81
COMEDY of ERRORS ..... Lucinda/Antipholus of S. ...3:30 93
CYMBELINE .... Cloton/Lord 3:30 68
WINTER'S TALE .... Hermione/Leontes 3:31 108
TITUS ANDRONICUS .... 3M 3:32 119
HAMLET .... 1st Clown/2nd Clown 3:36 69
TWO GENTLEMEN ...... Julia/Silvia 3:36 92
MERCHANT of VENICE .. Bassanio/Antonio 3:39 77
TWELFTH NIGHT .... Viola/Orsino 3:40 106
HAMLET .... Player Queen/Player King .3:42 95
HENRY VI, Part I .... Joan/Charles 3:43 96
MACBETH .... Lady Macbeth/Macbeth ...3:43 98
MUCH ADO .... Don John/Conrade 3:45 78
TAMING of the SHREW ... Lucentio/Tranio 3:45 81
TWELFTH NIGHT .... Viola/[Feste] ....3:45 . 92, 107
TWELFTH NIGHT .... 3M, [2M, 1W] 3:45 120
ALL'S WELL .... Diana/Bertram 3:48 93
HENRY VIII .... Anne/Old Lady 3:48 90
RICHARD III .... Richard/Buckingham 3:48 80

MEASURE for MEASURE . Isabell/Lucio 3:49 99
HENRY IV, Part II .... Henry/Warwick 3:51 72
AS YOU LIKE IT .... 3M 3:54 109
RICHARD III .... Queen Elizabeth/Richard .. 3:54 104
TWELFTH NIGHT .... Viola/Olivia 3:54 92
ANTONY & CLEOPATRA. Antony/Enobarbus 3:57 65
AS YOU LIKE IT .... Touchstone/Corin 4:00 65
HENRY VI, Part III .... 3M 4:00 114
KING LEAR .... Edgar/Gloucester 4:00 76
ROMEO & JULIET .... Romeo/Fr. Laurence 4:00 81
ROMEO & JULIET .... Juliet/Nurse 4:00 91
AS YOU LIKE IT .... Oliver/Charles 4:03 65
RICHARD II .... Queen/Richard 4:03 103
TIMON OF ATHENS ..... Timon/Flavius 4:03 83
HAMLET .... Ophelia/Hamlet 4:04 95
HENRY V .... 3M [2M, 1W] 4:06 113
MACBETH .... Lady Macbeth/Macbeth ... 4:06 98
OTHELLO .... Iago/Roderigo 4:06 79
MACBETH .... 3M 4:07 115
ROMEO & JULIET .... Juliet/Fr. Laurence 4:07 104
CORIOLANUS .... Brutus/Sicinius .... 4:08 .. 90, 94
CORIOLANUS .... [Brutus]/[Sicinius] 4:08 67
RICHARD II .... Bolingbrooke/York 4:08 80
HAMLET .... Hamlet/Ros. & Guild. 4:09 69
HENRY VI, Part III .... 3M 4:09 114
TROILUS & CRESSIDA ... Aeneas/Agamemnon 4:09 83
WINTERS TALE .... 2M, 1W [1M, 2W] 4:09 121
TROILUS & CRESSIDA ... Ulysses/Nestor 4:10 83
TWO NOBLE KINSMEN .. Arcite/Palamon 4:10 85
MUCH ADO .... Beatrice/Benedick 4:12 102
WINTER'S TALE .... Shepherd/Clown 4:15 87
HENRY VI, Part I .... Margaret/Suffolk 4:18 96
MERCHANT of VENICE .. Portia/Shylock 4:19 100
MACBETH .... 1M,2W .... 4:20 ✗ .. 115
MERCHANT of VENICE .. Launcelot/Gobbo 4:21 77
TAMING of the SHREW ... 3M 4:21 118
HENRY VIII .... Two Gentlemen 4:24 74
HENRY VIII .... [Two Gentlemen] .... 4:24 .. 90, 97
KING JOHN .... John/Hubert 4:25 75
THE TEMPEST .... Miranda/Ferdinand 4:25 105
HAMLET .... Hamlet/1st Clown 4:27 69
TAMING of the SHREW ... 2M, 1W 4:27 119
HAMLET .... Hamlet/Polonius 4:28 68
HENRY VI, Part II .... Cade/Iden 4:30 73
TWO GENTLEMEN ...... 2M, 1W [1M, 2W] 4:30 121
HENRY V .... 3M 4:33 112
TROILUS & CRESSIDA ... Troilus/Pandarus 4:33 83
CORIOLANUS .... Cominius/Coriolanus 4:35 66
HENRY IV, Part II .... 3M 4:36 112

TWO GENTLEMEN ...... [Speed]/Proteus 4:36 107
TWO GENTLEMEN ...... Proteus/Speed 4:36 84
WINTER'S TALE .... Paulina/Leontes 4:37 108
ANTONY & CLEOPATRA . Cleopatra/Antony 4:38 93
HENRY VI, Part III .... Henry/Gloucester 4:38 73
ALL'S WELL .... Parolles/Lafeu 4:39 65
HENRY VI, Part I .... 2M, 1W 4:39 113
TWO GENTLEMEN ...... Proteus/Valentine 4:39 84
HENRY IV, Part II .... 2M, 1W 4:40 111
HENRY VI, Part III .... 3M 4:42 113
MUCH ADO .... 2M, 1W [1M, 2W] 4:42 116
OTHELLO .... Desdemona/Othello 4:42 103
HENRY V .... 3M 4:43 113
HENRY IV, Part I .... 2M, 1W 4:44 111
AS YOU LIKE IT .... Celia/Rosalind 4:45 89
HENRY VIII .... Katherine/Griffith 4:45 97
MERCHANT of VENICE .. 2M, 1W 4:45 115
MUCH ADO .... 3W 4:45 117
CORIOLANUS .... Coriolanus/Aufidius 4:48 67
KING LEAR .... 3M [2M, 1W] 4:48 115
OTHELLO .... Emilia/Desdemona .... 4:48 ✘ ... 91
COMEDY OF ERRORS .... 2M, 1W 4:51 109
HAMLET .... Hamlet/Horatio 4:51 68
RICHARD III .... 4M [2M, 2W] 4:51 129
CORIOLANUS .... 3M [3W; 1M,2W; 2M,1W] . 4:54 109
TEMPEST .... Antonio/Sebastian 4:54 82
TWO GENTLEMEN ...... [Speed]/Valentine .... 4:54 .. 84,107
MERRY WIVES .... Falstaff/Ford 4:55 78
COMEDY OF ERRORS .... Antipholus/Dromio of S. .. 4:57 66
MEASURE for MEASURE . Isabell/Claudio 4:57 99
HENRY VI, Part II .... Queen Margaret/Suffolk ... 5:00 97
MUCH ADO .... 3M 5:00 117
TWO GENTLEMEN ...... 2M, 2W 5:06 131
ALL'S WELL .... 4W 5:09 123
JULIUS CAESAR .... 2M, 1W 5:09 114
HENRY VI, Part II .... Jack Cade/Lord Say 5:12 73
MIDSUMMER .... 3M, 1W 5:18 127
TIMON of ATHENS ...... Timon/Flavius 5:24 82
TWO GENTLEMEN ...... 3M 5:27 121
WINTER'S TALE .... Autolycus/Clown 5:27 87
COMEDY OF ERRORS .... Antipholus/Dromio of S. .. 5:30 66
HENRY IV, Part II .... 3M 5:30 111
HENRY VI, Part III .... 4M 5:30 124
OTHELLO .... Iago/Cassio 5:30 79
ROMEO & JULIET .... Juliet/Nurse 5:30 91
TAMING of the SHREW ... Katharina/Petruchio ...... 5:30 ✘ .. 105
HAMLET .... Hamlet/Osric 5:31 69
MEASURE for MEASURE . Duke/Lucio 5:31 76
ALL'S WELL .... Helena/King 5:36 93

HAMLET . . . . Hamlet/Ghost 5:36 68
MERRY WIVES . . . . Mrs. Page/Mrs. Ford 5:36 91
TWO GENTLEMEN . . . . . . 2M, 2W [1M, 3W] 5:36 131
ROMEO & JULIET . . . . Romeo/Mercutio 5:42 80
WINTER'S TALE . . . . Polixenes/Camillo 5:45 86
HENRY IV, Part II . . . . Prince Hal/Poins 5:48 71
CYMBELINE . . . . Iachimo/Posthumus 5:51 68
HENRY IV, Part I . . . . Prince Hal/Falstaff 5:51 69
TWO GENTLEMEN . . . . . . [Speed]/Launce . . . . 5:51 . . 85,107
CYMBELINE . . . . Iachimo/Posthumus 5:52 67
HENRY IV, Part I . . . . 3M 5:54 111
KING JOHN . . . . 4M [3M, 1W] 5:54 126
TEMPEST . . . . [Ariel]/Prospero . . . . 5:54 . . 81,105
TIMON OF ATHENS . . . . . 3M 5:55 119
HENRY VIII . . . . 3M 5:57 114
HAMLET . . . . 3M 6:00 109
CORIOLANUS . . . . Menenius/First Citizen 6:09 66
TWELFTH NIGHT . . . . Malvolio/[Feste] . . . . 6:09 . 84, 107
TROILUS & CRESSIDA . . . Cressida/Troilus 6:10 106
CORIOLANUS . . . . 3W 6:12 109
MIDSUMMER . . . . 1M,2W 6:12 116
TWO NOBLE KINSMEN . . Arcite/Palamon 6:12 85
MERCHANT of VENICE . . Shylock/Antonio 6:13 77
AS YOU LIKE IT . . . . 2M, 2W 6:15 123
TROILUS & CRESSIDA . . . 2M,1W 6:15 119
TEMPEST . . . . 3M, 1W [2M, 2W] 6:21 130
TWELFTH NIGHT . . . . 2M,1W [1M,2W] 6:21 121
MIDSUMMER . . . . [Puck]/Oberon . . . . 6:22 . . 78,101
LOVE'S LABOURS . . . . Armado/[Moth] . . . . 6:27 . . 76, 98
TITUS ANDRONICUS . . . . 3M, 1W [2M, 2W] 6:27 130
TWO NOBLE KINSMEN . . Arcite/Palamon 6:33 86
KING JOHN . . . . [Arthur]/Hubert . . . . 6:39 . . 75, 98
HENRY IV, Part II . . . . Henry/Prince Hal 6:42 72
HENRY IV, Part II . . . . 2M, 2W 6:42 124
MACBETH . . . . 1M, 3W 6:42 127
TROILUS & CRESSIDA . . . 2M, 1W 6:42 120
WINTER'S TALE . . . . Autolycus/Clown 6:45 87
KING JOHN . . . . 3M, 1W 6:46 125
HAMLET . . . . 2M, 1W 6:48 110
TROILUS & CRESSIDA . . . 3M 6:48 119
TWO GENTLEMEN . . . . . . Duke/Valentine 6:51 85
MACBETH . . . . Macduff/Malcolm 6:57 76
MERRY WIVES . . . . Falstaff/Ford 6:57 78
TAMING of the SHREW . . . 3M 7:00 118
TWO GENTLEMEN . . . . . . Julia/Lucetta 7:00 92
TROILUS & CRESSIDA . . . Ulysses/Achilles 7:05 83
ROMEO & JULIET . . . . 4M 7:06 130
TEMPEST . . . . 3M, 1W [2M, 2W] 7:06 130
ALL'S WELL . . . . Helena/Parolles 7:09 93

HENRY VI, Part I .... Talbot/John 7:09 73
LOVE'S LABOURS .... 3M [2M, 1W] 7:09 115
TITUS ANDRONICUS .... Tamora/Titus 7:09 105
TWELFTH NIGHT .... Viola/Olivia 7:09 91
KING LEAR .... Edmund/Gloucester 7:15 75
MERCHANT of VENICE .. Portia/Nerissa 7:18 90
ROMEO & JULIET .... 1M,2W 7:18 118
TAMING of the SHREW ... 4m [3M, 1W; 2M, 2W] 7:18 130
PERICLES .... Antiochus/Pericles 7:21 79
HENRY V .... Henry/Michael Williams .. 7:24 72
MEASURE for MEASURE . Isabell/Angelo 7:25 99
CORIOLANUS .... Brutus/Sicinius 7:26 67
KING JOHN .... 4M 7:27 125
RICHARD III .... Richard/Buckingham 7:30 80
MEASURE for MEASURE . Duke/Provost 7:33 77
TWELFTH NIGHT .... 2M, 1W 7:33 120
HENRY IV, Part I .... Lady Percy/Hotspur 7:36 95
HENRY IV, Part I .... 3M 7:36 110
WINTER'S TALE .... Leontes/Camillo 7:39 86
HENRY IV, Part II .... Northumberland/Morton .. 7:45 72
HENRY IV, Part II .... Falstaff/Justice 7:48 71
MERRY WIVES .... 1M,2W 7:48 116
HAMLET .... 3M 7:60 109
HENRY IV, Part I .... Prince Hal/Falstaff 8:00 71
JULIUS CAESAR .... Cassius/Brutus 8:00 74
RICHARD II .... 3M 8:00 117
PERICLES .... 2M, 2W 8:05 128
MEASURE for MEASURE . Isabell/Angelo 8:24 99
MUCH ADO .... 3M 8:24 116
HENRY V .... 3M 8:27 112
HENRY IV, Part I .... 2M, 1W 8:30 111
OTHELLO .... 2M, 2W 8:33 128
MUCH ADO .... Beatrice/Benedick 8:36 102
PERICLES .... 4M 8:36 128
HENRY IV, Part I .... Hotspur/Worcester 8:47 70
KING LEAR .... 4M .... 8:48(+) . 126
RICHARD II .... 3M, 1W [2M, 2W] 9:00 128
HENRY IV, Part I .... Hal/Falstaff 9:09 70
HENRY VIII .... 5M 9:09 125
ROMEO & JULIET .... 1M, 3W 9:09 130
OTHELLO .... 3M 9:12 117
HENRY V .... 3M 9:15 113
HENRY VIII .... Norfolk/Buckingham 9:18 74
MERCHANT of VENICE .. Portia/Bassanio 9:21 100
RICHARD II .... 3M 9:24 117
RICHARD III .... Lady Anne/Richard ...... 9:24 ✗ .. 104
MACBETH .... Lady Macbeth/Macbeth ... 9:25 98
ROMEO & JULIET .... Juliet/Romeo .... 9:28 ✗ .. 104
HENRY IV, Part I .... 3M 9:30 110

RICHARD III	3M	9:30	118
KING LEAR	3M	9:33	115
TWO NOBLE KINSMEN	Arcite/Palamon	9:33	85
TEMPEST	3M	9:36	119
CORIOLANUS	Volumnia/Coriolanus	9:45	94
RICHARD III	1M, 3W	9:45	129
CYMBELINE	Imogen/Pisanio	9:46	94
HENRY V	3M, 1W	9:51	124
MUCH ADO	4M	10:05	127
CYMBELINE	Imogen/Iachimo	10:22	94
HAMLET	Gertrude/Hamlet	10:30 ✗	95
PERICLES	2M, 2W	10:36	128
TROILUS & CRESSIDA	2M, 1W	10:39	120
HENRY VIII	3M, 1W	10:42	125
HENRY IV, Part II	3M	11:05	112
MIDSUMMER	2M, 2W	11:09	127
TIMON of ATHENS	Timon/Apemantus	11:09	82
OTHELLO	Desdemona/Othello	11:13	103
HAMLET	2M, 2W	11:18	124
JULIUS CAESAR	Cassius/Brutus	11:18 ✗	74
RICHARD III	Queen Elizabeth/Richard	11:48	104
HENRY IV, Part I	3M	12:00	110
MEASURE for MEAS.	4M	12:09	127
CORIOLANUS	5M [4M, 1W; 3M, 2W]	12:12	123
AS YOU LIKE IT	Celia/Rosalind	12:15	89
ANTONY & CLEO.	4M	12:30	123
MERRY WIVES	Falstaff/Ford	13:24	78
HAMLET	3M	13:30	110
RICHARD III	2M, 2W	13:45	129
TROILUS & CRESSIDA	Cressida/Pandarus	13:45	106
TWO NOBLE KINSMEN	3M, 1W [2M, 2W; 1M, 3W]	15:30	132
MEASURE for MEASURE	Isabell/Angelo	15:49	99
RICHARD II	3M	17:24	118
MERCHANT of VENICE	Portia/Bassanio	17:39	101
OTHELLO	Iago/Othello	17:42	79
LOVE'S LABOURS	4M	18:12	126
HENRY IV, Part I	Falstaff/Prince Hal	18:39	71
WINTER'S TALE	3M, 1W	19:12	132
TROILUS & CRESSIDA	2M, 1W	19:33	120
TROILUS & CRESSIDA	4M	19:36	131
TWELFTH NIGHT	4M, 1W [3M,2W]	21:48	131
TWO NOBLE KINSMEN	Arcite/Palomon	25:00	86

INDEX: All Pieces, by Play Title

(First monologues, then scenes, in alphabetical order by character name. Listings in [brackets] indicate switched gender. Chestnuts ✘ are not shown here.)

All's Well That Ends Well

Helena	1:21	4
King of France	2:33	34
Bertram/Diana	3:48	93
Diana/Helena/Mariana/Widow	5:09	123
Helena/King of France	5:36	93
Helena/Parolles	7:09	93
Lafeu/Parolles	4:39	65

Antony and Cleopatra

Antony	1:12	20
Caesar	1:23	25
Cleopatra	1:30, 1:09, 1:06	1
Cleopatra	1:41	2
Enobarbus	2:18	31
Agrippa/Antony/Caesar/Enobarbus	12:30	123
Antony/Cleopatra	2:59, 4:38	93
Antony/Enobarbus	3:57	65
Enobarbus/Menas	3:03	65

As You Like It

Adam	2:39	19
Duke Senior	1:09	30
Jaques	2:27, 1:18	44
Lord	1:57	46
Oliver	2:21	49
Phebe	1:00, 1:54	10
Rosalind	1:48, 1:12, 2:24, 2:48	15
Rosalind	1:27	15
Touchstone	1:24, 1:48	60
Amiens/Jaques	3:15	65
Celia/LeBeau/Rosalind/Touchstone	6:15	123
Celia/Rosalind	2:06, 2:27, 2:57, 4:45, 12:15	89
Charles/Oliver	4:03	65
Corin/Touchstone	4:00	65
Duke Senior/Jaques/Orlando	3:54	109
Jaques/Orlando	2:12	66

Comedy of Errors

Adriana	1:51	1
Antipholus of Syracuse	1:12	20
Luciana	1:24	8
Antipholus/Dromio of Syracuse	4:57, 5:30	66
Antipholus of Syracuse/Luciana	3:30	93
Antipholus/Dromio of S./Courtesan	4:51	109

Coriolanus

Aufidius	1:33, 2:18	21
Cominius	2:18	29
Coriolanus	1:45, 1:51	29
Menenius	3:39, 2:33	48
Volumnia	4:23, 2:49	16
Adrian/Nicanor	2:85	67
Aufidius/Coriolanus	4:48	67
Aufidius/Coriolanus/3 Servants	12:12	123
Brutus/Sicinius	3:18	66
Brutus/Sicinius	7:26	67
[Brutus]/[Sicinius]	4:08	67, [90], [94]
Cominius/Coriolanus	4:35	66
Cominius/Menenius	2:27	67
Coriolanus/Volumnia	9:45	94
First Citizen/Menenius	6:09	66
Three Servants	4:54	109
Valeria/Virgilia/Volumnia	6:12	109

Cymbeline

Belarius	4:21	22
Cloten	1:24	29
Iachimo	2:39, 2:03	43
Imogen	4:26, 1:21, 2:06	5
Posthumus	1:39, 1:45	51
Posthumus	2:24, 1:21	52
Cloten/Imogen	2:54	94
Cloten/Lord	3:30	68
Imogen/Iachimo	10:22	94
Iachimo/Posthumus	5:52	67
Iachimo/Posthumus	5:51	68
Imogen/Pisanio	9:46	94

Hamlet

Claudius	1:54	28
[First Player]	2:56	[18], 33
Ghost	3:59	34
Hamlet	2:57, 1:39, 1:30, 4:24, 4:24, 2:30, 1:40	36
Hamlet	1:12, 2:00, 1:45, 1:33	37
Ophelia	3:45	9
Polonius	3:46	51
1st Clown/2nd Clown	3:36	69
Bernardo/Horatio/Marcellus	(6:00) 7:60	109
Claudius/Gertrude/Laertes/Ophelia	11:18	124
Claudius/Hamlet	2:42	69
Gertrude/Hamlet	10:30	95
Hamlet/1st Clown	4:27	69
Hamlet/Ghost	5:36	68
Hamlet/Horatio	4:51	68

Hamlet/Ophelia 4:04 95
Hamlet/Osric 5:31 69
Hamlet/Polonius 4:28 68
Hamlet/Polonius/Ros. & Guild. 13:30 110
Hamlet/Ros. & Guild. 4:09 69
Laertes/Ophelia/Polonius 6:48 110
Ophelia/Polonius 2:17 95
Player King/Player Queen 3:42 95

Henry IV, Part I
Falstaff 1:09, 1:15 31
Falstaff 1:03, 0:48, 2:03 32
Henry IV 1:39, 5:48 38
Hotspur 1:30, 3:00, 2:03, 1:54 42
Lady Percy 1:27 8
Prince Hal 1:09, 1:42, 1:33 52
Falstaff/Mistress Quickly 2:06 95
Falstaff/Prince Hal 5:51 69
Falstaff/Prince Hal 9:09 70
Falstaff/Prince Hal 18:39, 8:00 71
Falstaff/Prince Hal/Mistress Quickly 4:44, 8:30 111
Falstaff/Prince Hal/Poins . . . . 12:00 or 7:36 110
Gadshill/Chamberlain 2:45 70
Glendower/Hotspur/Mortimer 9:30 110
Henry IV/Prince Hal/Worcester 5:54 111
Hotspur/Lady Percy 7:36 95
Hotspur/Prince Hal 2:03 71
Hotspur/Worcester 8:47 70
Prince Hal/Poins 3:06 70

Henry IV, Part II
[Epilogue] . . . . 1:51 . . [17], 31
Falstaff 2:09, 1:21, 2:15, 1:48 32
Henry IV . . . . 1:33, 1:45, 3:18, 1:15, 1:30, ... 38
Henry IV 2:09, 2:18, 1:09 39
Lady Percy 1:51 8
Mistress Quickly 1:03 9
Mistress Quickly 1:18 8
Prince Hal 1:24 52
Prince Hal 1:57, 1:18, 2:12 53
[Rumour] . . . . 2:00 . . [18], 58
Shallow 2:18 58
Warwick 1:36 61
Davy/Falstaff/Shallow 4:36 112
Doll/Falstaff/Pistol/Quickly 6:42 124
Falstaff/Justice 7:48 71
Falstaff/Justice/Quickly 4:40 111
Hastings/Bardolph/York 5:30 111
Henry/Prince Hal 6:42 72
Henry/Warwick 3:51 72

Morton/Northumberland 7:45 73
Mowbray/Westmoreland/York. 11:05 112
Poins/Prince Hal 5:48 71

Henry V
[Boy] . . . . 1:27 . . [17], 23
Burgundy. 2:15 25
Canterbury 3:09 26
[Chorus] . . . . 2:39, 1:45, 2:06, 1:42 . . [17], 27
[Chorus] . . . . 2:15 . . [17], 28
Constable of France 1:09 29
Exeter 1:51, 1:18 31
Henry V 2:36, 4:42 39
Henry V 3:34, 1:48, 1:42, 2:09, 2:06, 2:24 40
Henry V 5:57 41
Quickly 1:00 9
Bardolph/Nym/Pistol/Quickly 9:51 124
[Boy]/Pistol/Soldier 4:06 113
Dauphin/France/Orleans 8:27 112
Fluellen/Gower/Pistol 4:33 112
Fluellen/Gower/Pistol 4:43, 9:15 113
Henry/Michael Williams 7:24 72
Henry/Montjoy 2:48 72
Katharine/Alice 3:12 90

Henry VI, Part I
Joan La Pucelle. 1:42, 1:27 6
Messenger 1:54 48
Old Talbot 1:36 49
Charles/Joan 3:43 96
Joan/Shepherd/Warwick(York) 4:39 113
Joan/Warwick(York) 3:01 96
Margaret/Suffolk 4:18 96
Talbot/John 7:09 72

Henry VI, Part II
Cade 1:18, 0:51, 1:15 25
Captain 1:42 26
Clifford 1:45 28
Duchess of Gloucester 1:54 3
Gloucester 1:30, 1:27 35
Henry VI 1:15 38
Queen Margaret 1:54, 2:00 12
Queen Margaret 1:45, 3:15 13
Suffolk 2:33 58
Suffolk 2:12 59
York 2:39, 2:18 62
Cade/Iden 4:30 73
Cade/Lord Say 5:12 73
Duchess/Duke of Gloucester 2:43 96

Duchess/Hume 2:24 96
Queen Margaret/Suffolk 5:00 97

Henry VI, Part III
Clarence 1:06 28
Clifford 1:42 28
Clifford 1:30 29
Gloucester 3:36, 1:39 35
Henry VI 1:54, 2:42, 2:13 41
Messenger 1:03 48
Queen Margaret 0:51, 2:09, 1:54, 1:21 13
Warwick 1:54, 1:12 61
York 1:18, 2:48 62
Clifford/Edward/Richard/Warwick 5:30 124
Clifford/Rutland 2:09 73
Edward/Lady Grey 3:18 97
Edward/Messenger/Richard 4:42 113
Edward/Richard/Warwick 4:00 114
Henry/Father/Son 4:09 114
Henry/Gloucester 4:38 73

Henry VIII
Buckingham 3:35, 2:09 24
Cranmer 1:27 29
Cranmer 2:27 30
Gentleman 1:39 34
Henry VIII 3:57 41
Henry VIII 2:54, 2:10 42
Norfolk 1:54 49
Porter's Man 1:09 51
[Prologue] . . . . 1:36 . . [18], 53
Queen Katharine 1:06, 2:15 11
Queen Katharine 3:49, 2:12, 3:47 12
Wolsey 1:06, 1:09, 0:51, 1:15 61
Wolsey 3:06 62
Anne/Old Lady 3:48 90
Chamberlain/Lovell/Sands 3:21 114
Chancellor/Cranmer/Cromwell/
    Gardiner/Henry 9:09 125
Henry/Katharine/Surveyor/Wolsey 10:42 125
Henry/Wolsey 3:25 74
Katherine/Griffith 4:45 97
Norfolk/Buckingham 9:18 74
Porter/Porter's Man 3:24 74
Suffolk/Surrey/Wolsey 5:57 114
[Two Gentlemen] . . . . 4:24 74,[90],[97]

Julius Caesar
Antony 2:09, 8:00, 1:45, 1:06 20
Brutus 1:21, 1:06, 2:54, 2:21 23

Caesar 1:30, 1:03 26
Casca 1:36, 1:27 26
Cassius 3:30, 3:27 27
Marullus 1:12 47
Portia 1:09, 2:51 10
Brutus/Cassius 8:00, 11:18 74
Caesar/Calpurnia 2:27 97
Caesar/Calpurnia/Decius 5:09 114

King John
(Philip the) Bastard 2:03, 1:54 21
(Philip the) Bastard 2:15, 1:57 22
Constance 3:14, 2:12, 6:45, 3:31 2
King John 2:42, 2:06 44
Lewis 1:57 46
Melun 1:57 48
Pandulph 2:12 50
[Arthur]/Hubert . . . . 6:39 . . 75, [98]
Bastard/Elinor/John/Robert 6:46 125
Bastard/Henry/John/Salisbury 5:54 126
Bastard/Hubert/Pembroke/Salisbury 7:27 125
Hubert/John 4:25 75
Hubert/Philip 2:12 75
Salisbury/Lewis 3:13 75

King Lear
Cordelia 0:51 3
Edgar 1:03 30
Edmund 1:06 30
Lear 1:07, 1:36, 1:09, 4:24 45
Cordelia/Lear 2:35 98
Edgar/[Fool]/Kent/Lear . . . . 8:48 (or longer) 126
Edgar/Gloucester/Lear 9:33 115
Edmund/Gloucester 2:40, 4:00, 7:156
[Fool]/Kent/Lear 4:48 115
[Fool]/Lear . . . . 2:21 . . 75, [98]
Regan/Lear 3:00 98

Love's Labours Lost
Armado 1:03 21
Biron (Berowne) 1:33, 3:48 23
Armado/Costard/[Moth] 7:09 115
Armado/[Moth] . . . . 6:27 . . 76, [98]
Biron/Dumain/King/Longaville 18:12 126

Macbeth
Lady Macbeth 1:00, 2:23 8
Macbeth 1:24 46
Macbeth 1:42, 1:15, 1:30 47
Porter 1:09 51

[Doctor]/Gentlewoman/Lady Macbeth 4:20 115
Lady Macbeth/Macbeth 3:43, 4:06 98
Lady Macbeth/Macbeth 9:25 99
Macbeth/Macduff 1:42 76
Macduff/Malcolm 6:57 76
Macduff/Malcolm/Ross 4:07 115
Macbeth/3 Witches 6:42 127

Measure for Measure
Angelo 1:16 19
Claudio 1:51 28
Angelo/Isabell 7:25, 8:24, 15:49 99
Claudio/Isabell 4:57 99
Duke/Lucio 5:31 76
Duke/Provost 7:33 77
Elbow/Escalus/Froth/Pompey 12:09 127
Isabella/Lucio 3:49 99

Merchant of Venice
Aragon 3:08 20
Launcelot 1:39 45
Lorenzo 1:45 46
Morocco 3:06 49
Portia 1:09, 1:12 10
Portia 2:21, 1:06 11
Shylock 2:51, 1:24, 1:33 58
Antonio/Bassanio 3:39 77
Antonio/Shylock 6:13 77
Bassanio/Portia 2:03, 2:57, 3:17, 9:21 100
Bassanio/Portia 17:39 101
Gobbo/Launcelot 4:21 77
Jessica/Lorenzo 2:50 100
Jessica/Launcelot/Lorenzo 4:45 115
Nerissa/Portia 7:18 90
Portia/Shylock 4:19 100
Salanio/Salarino 2:40 77

Merry Wives of Windsor
Falstaff 3:06 33
Ford 1:27 33
Mistress Quickly 3:12 9
Falstaff/Ford 4:55, 6:57, 13:24 78
Falstaff/Mrs. Ford/Mrs. Page 7:48 116
Mrs. Ford/Mrs. Page 5:36 91

A Midsummer Night's Dream
Helena 1:18, 3:21 4
Oberon 2:00 49
[Puck] . . . . 1:26 . . [18], 54
Titania 1:51 16

Demetrius/Helena 2:15, 2:51 101
Demetrius/Helena/Hermia/Lysander 11:09 127
[Fairy]/[Puck] . . . . 2:47 [78],[91],101
Hermia/Lysander 2:36, 2:51 101
Helena/Hermia/Lysander 6:12 116
Egeus/Hermia/Lysander/Theseus 5:18 127
Oberon/[Puck] . . . . 6:22 . [78], 101

Much Ado About Nothing
Benedick 1:57, 1:24, 1:36 22
Dogberry 0:45 30
Don John 1:27 30
Friar Francis 1:42 34
Leonato 1:12, 1:51 46
Beatrice/Benedick 1:39, 2:45, 4:12, 8:36 102
Beatrice/Leonato/[Messenger] 4:42 116
Beatrice/Hero/Margaret 4:45 117
Benedick/Claudio/Don Pedro 8:24 116
Benedick/Claudio/Don Pedro 5:00 117
Benedick/Claudio/Don Pedro/Leonato 10:05 127
Don John/Conrade 3:45 78

Othello
Emelia 1:36 4
Iago 2:43, 4:21, 4:24 43
Iago 1:21, 1:20 44
Othello 3:03, 1:06 50
Brabantio/Iago/Roderigo 9:12 117
Desdemona/Emilia 4:48 91
Desdemona/Emilia/Iago/Othello 8:33 128
Desdemona/Othello 3:12, 3:19, 4:42 102
Desdemona/Othello 11:13 103
Iago/Cassio 5:30 79
Iago/Othello 17:42 79
Iago/Roderigo 4:06 79

Pericles
Gower 1:41 35
Antiochus/Pericles 7:21 79
Bawd/Bould/Marina/Pandar 8:05 128
Bawd/Bould/Lysimachus/Marina 10:36 128
Dionyzia/Cleon 2:33 103
Pericles/3 Fishermen 8:36 128

Richard II
Bolingbrooke 1:30, 1:51 23
Carlisle 1:48 26
Duchess of Gloucester 2:57 3
Gardener 2:09 34
Gaunt 1:54 34

Queen 1:13 11
Richard II 2:48, 2:24, 2:51, 2:30 54
Richard II 5:15, 3:16, 1:45, 1:06, 5:54 55
York 2:36 62
York 2:00, 1:54 63
Aumerle/Bolingbrooke/Duke & Duchess of York . 9:00 . . . 128
Bolingbrooke/Gaunt 2:51 79
Bolingbrooke/Mowbray/Richard 8:00, 9:24 117
Bolingbrooke/Mowbray/Richard 17:24 118
Bolingbrooke/York 4:08 80
Gardener/Queen 2:00 103
Queen/Richard 4:03 103
Richard/Scroop 3:15 80

Richard III
Buckingham 1:54, 3:03 24
Buckingham 1:21 25
Clarence 3:17 28
Duchess of York 1:18, 1:21 3
Edward 1:36 31
Hastings 1:15 37
Lady Anne 1:36, 1:24 1
Queen Elizabeth 1:00 11
Queen Margaret 2:03, 2:00, 2:51, 1:21, 0:54 14
Queen Margaret 4:03 15
Richard III 1:09, 1:18, 2:03, 1:51, 1:39 56
Richard III 2:33, 1:03, 2:18, 1:30, 1:54 57
Richmond 1:45 57
Tyrrel 1:09 60
Buckingham/Richard 3:48, 7:30 80
Buckingham/[York]/Gloucester/[Prince Edward] . 4:51 . . . 129
Clarence/2 Murderers 9:30 118
Duchess of York/Queen Elizabeth/
Queen Margaret/Richard 9:45 129
Gloucester/Queen Elizabeth/
Queen Margaret/Rivers 13:45 129
Lady Anne/Richard 9:24 103
Queen Elizabeth/Richard 3:54, 11:48 104

Romeo and Juliet
Fr. Laurence 1:30 33
Fr. Laurence 2:33 34
Juliet 2:15, 2:55, 1:39 7
Mercutio 2:30 48
Nurse 2:15 9
Romeo 2:21 57
Benvolio/Mercutio/Romeo/Tybalt 7:06 130
Benvolio/Romeo/Servant 3:27 118
Capulet/Juliet/Lady Capulet 7:18 118
Capulet/Juliet/Lady Capulet/Nurse 9:09 130

Fr. Laurence/Juliet 4:07 104
Fr. Laurence/Romeo 4:00, 3:21 81
Gregory/Sampson 2:30 80
Juliet/Nurse 5:30, 4:00 91
Juliet/Romeo 3:08, 9:28 104
Mercutio/Romeo 5:42 80
Mercutio/Romeo 3:29 81
Nurse/Romeo 3:00 104

Sir Thomas More (fragment)
More 4:03 48

The Taming of the Shrew
Katharina 2:12 7
Petruchio 1:20 51
Baptista/Gremio/Tranio 4:21 118
Bianca/Hortensio/Lucentio 4:27 118
Grumio/Hortensio/Petruchio 7:00 119
Katharina/Petruchio 5:30 105
Lucentio/Tranio 3:45 81
Lord/[Page]/[Servant]/Sly 7:18 130

The Tempest
Prospero 0:48, 2:04 53
Antonio/Sebastian 4:54 82
Ariel/Ferdinand/Miranda/Prospero. . . . . 6:21 or 7:06 130
[Ariel]/Prospero . . . . 5:54 . 81, [105]
Caliban/Prospero 2:48 81
Caliban/Stephano/Trinculo 9:36 119
Miranda/Ferdinand 4:25 105

Timon of Athens
Flavius 1:24 33
Timon 2:03, 2:30, 1:27, 2:21 59
Apemantus/Timon 11:09 82
Flaminius/Lucullus 3:03 82
Flavius/Timon 5:24 82
Flavius/Timon 4:03 83
Painter/Poet/Timon 5:55 119
Sepromonius/Servant 2:06 82

Titus Andronicus
Aaron 1:09 19
Marcus 2:21 47
Titus 2:09, 2:00 59
Aaron/Tamora 2:42 105
Aaron/Chiron/Demetrius 3:32 119
Lavinia/Marcus/Titus/[Young Lucius] 6:27 130
Tamora/Titus 7:09 105

Troilus and Cressida

Aeneas 1:22 19
Agamemnon 1:28 19
Ulysses 2:17, 3:06, 6:33 60
Achilles/Ajax/Thersites 6:48 119
Achilles/Ulysses 7:05 83
Aeneas/Agamemnon 4:09 83
Aeneas/Agamemnon/Nestor/Ulysses 19:36 131
Cressida/Pandarus 13:45 105
Cressida/Pandarus/Troilus 6:42, 10:39, 19:33 120
Cressida/Troilus 6:10 106
Helen/Pandarus/Paris 6:15 119
Nestor/Ulysses 4:10 83
Pandarus/[Servant] . . . . 2:15 . 83, [106]
Pandarus/Troilus 4:33 83

Twelfth Night
Malvolio 5:48 47
Orsino 1:49 50
Viola 1:15, 0:58 16
Andrew/[Feste]/Toby 3:45 120
Andrew/Feste/Malvolio/Maria/Toby 21:48 131
Andrew/Maria/Toby 7:33 120
Andrew/Toby 3:21 83
Captain/Viola 3:00 106
[Feste]/Malvolio . . . . 6:09 . 84, [107]
Feste/Maria 2:00 106
[Feste]/Orsino/Viola 6:21 121
[Feste]/Viola . . . . 3:45 . [92], 107
Maria/Toby 2:18 106
Olivia/Viola 7:09 91
Olivia/Viola 3:54 92
Orsino/Viola 3:40 106

The Two Gentlemen of Verona
Julia 1:18, 1:21 7
Launce 1:45 44
Launce 2:12 45
Proteus 2:09 54
Duke/Valentine 6:51 85
[Host]/Julia/Proteus/Silvia 5:36 131
Julia/Lucetta 7:00 92
Julia/Proteus/Silvia/Valentine 5:06 131
Julia/Silvia 3:36 92
Launce/Proteus/Valentine 5:27 121
[Launce]/[Speed] . . . . 3:06 84,[92],[107]
Launce/[Speed] . . . . 5:51 . 85, [107]
Proteus/[Speed] . . . . 4:36 . 84, [107]
Proteus/Valentine 3:27, 4:39 84
Silvia/[Speed]/Valentine 4:30 121
[Speed]/Valentine . . . . 4:54 . 84, [107]

The Two Noble Kinsmen
Arcite 1:45 21
Emilia 1:24 3
Emilia 3:00, 1:51 4
Jailer's Daughter 1:57, 1:39 5
Jailer's Daughter 1:18, 1:36, 6:48, 1:54 6
Palamon 3:24 50
[Pirithous] . . . . 1:48 . . [18], 51
Arcite/Palamon 2:39, 4:10, 6:12, 9:33 85
Arcite/Palamon 6:33, 25:00 86
[Doctor]/[Jailer]/Jailer's Daughter/Wooer 15:30 132

The Winter's Tale
Antigonus 2:09 19
Hermione 3:53 5
Paulina 2:39 9
[Archidamus]/[Camillo] . . . . 2:31 86,[92],[108]
Autolycus/Clown . . . . 6:45 or 5:27 87
Camillo/Hermione/Leontes/Polixenes 19:12 132
Camillo/Leontes 7:39 86
Camillo/Polixenes 5:45 86
[Cleomenes(Dion)]/Leontes/Paulina 4:09 121
Clown/Shepherd 4:15 87
Florizel/Perdita 2:43 108
Hermione/Leontes 3:31 108
Leontes/Paulina 4:37 108

INDEX: All Characters, by Age Range

*(Characters are grouped according to age range and gender.
Character name in boldface indicates that character has a
monologue; [brackets] indicate switched gender.)*

WOMEN: YOUNG ADULT
(age 15 - 25)

Anne - *Henry VIII*
Bianca - *Shrew*
[Boy] - *Henry V*
Celia - *As You Like It*
Cordelia - *King Lear*
Desdemona - *Othello*
Diana - *All's Well*
Emilia - 2 Noble Kinsmen
[Fairy] - *Midsummer*
Helena - *All's Well*
Helena - *Midsummer*
Hermia - *Midsummer*
Hero - *Much Ado*
Imogen - *Cymbeline*
Isabell - *Measure*
Jailer's Daughter - *2 Noble Kins.*
Jessica - *Merchant*
Joan La Pucelle - *Henry VI - I*
Juliet - *Romeo & Juliet*
Katharine - *Henry V*
Lady Anne - *Richard III*
Lady Percy - *Henry IV - I, II*
Lavinia - *Titus*
Marina - *Pericles*
Miranda - *Tempest*
[Moth] - *Love's Labours*
Nerissa - *Merchant*
Ophelia - *Hamlet*
Perdita - *Winter's Tale*
Phebe - *As You Like It*
Portia - *Merchant*
[Puck] - *Midsummer*
Rosalind - *As You Like It*
Viola - *12th Night*
[Young Lucius] - *Titus*

MEN: YOUNG ADULT
(age 15 - 25)

Arthur - *King John*
Bassanio - *Merchant*
Benvolio - *Romeo & Juliet*
Bertram - *All's Well*
Boy - *Henry V*
Claudio - *Measure*
Claudio - *Much Ado*
Florizel - *Winter's Tale*
Demetrius - *Midsummer*
Fairy - *Midsummer*
Ferdinand - *Tempest*

Froth - *Measure for Measure*
Hotspur - *Henry IV - I*
Launcelot - *Merchant*
Lorenzo - *Merchant*
Lucentio - *Shrew*
Lysander - *Midsummer*
Mercutio - *Romeo & Juliet*
Moth - *Love's Labours*
Orlando - *As You Like It*
Poins - *Henry IV - I*
Poins - *Henry IV - II*
Posthumus - *Cymbeline*
Prince Edward - *Richard III*
Prince Hal - *Henry IV - I, II*
Puck - *Midsummer*
Romeo - *Romeo & Juliet*
Rutland - *Henry VI - III*
Son - *Henry VI - III*
York - *Richard III*
Young Lucius - *Titus*

MEN: ADULT (age 25 - 45)

1st Clown - *Hamlet*
2nd Clown - *Hamlet*
Aaron - *Titus*
Achilles - *Troilus & Cressida*
Adrian - *Coriolanus*
Aeneas - *Troilus & Cressida*
Agamemnon - *Troilus & Cressida*
Agrippa - *Antony & Cleopatra*
Ajax - *Troilus & Cressida*
Amiens - *As You Like It*
Andrew - *12th Night*
Angelo - *Measure*
Antigonus - *Winter's Tale*
Antiochus - *Pericles*
Antipholus of Syracuse - *Errors*
Antonio - *Merchant*
Antonio - *Tempest*
Antony - *Antony & Cleopatra*
Antony - *Julius Caesar*
Apemantus - *Timon*
Aragon - *Merchant*
Archidamus - *Winter's Tale*
Arcite - *2 Noble Kinsmen*
Ariel - *Tempest*
Armado - *Love's Labours*
Aufidius - *Coriolanus*
Aumerle - *Richard II*
Autolycus - *Winter's Tale*
Baptista - *Shrew*
Bardolph - *Henry IV - II*

Bastard (Philip) - *King John*
Bardolph - *Henry V*
Benedick - *Much Ado*
Biron (Berowne) - *Love's Labours*
Bolingbrooke - *Richard II*
Bould - *Pericles*
Brutus - *Coriolanus*
Brutus - *Julius Caesar*
Buckingham - *Henry VIII*
Buckingham - *Richard III*
Burgundy - *Henry V*
Cade - *Henry VI - II*
Caesar - *Antony & Cleopatra*
Caliban - *Tempest*
Camillo - *Winter's Tale*
Canterbury - *Henry V*
Captain - *12th Night*
Captain - *Henry VI - II*
Capulet - *Romeo & Juliet*
Carlisle - *Richard II*
Casca - *Julius Caesar*
Cassio - *Othello*
Cassius - *Julius Caesar*
Chamberlain - *Henry IV - I*
Chamberlain - *Henry VIII*
Chancellor - *Henry VIII*
Charles - *As You Like It*
Charles - *Henry VI - I*
Chiron - *Titus*
Chorus - *Henry V*
Clarence - *Henry VI - III*
Clarence - *Richard III*
Claudius - *Hamlet*
Cleomenes/Dion - *Winter's Tale*
Cleon - *Pericles*
Clifford - *Henry VI - II, III*
Cloten - *Cymbeline*
Clown - *Winter's Tale*
Cominius - *Coriolanus*
Conrade - *Much Ado*
Constable of France - *Henry V*
Corin - *As You Like It*
Coriolanus - *Coriolanus*
Costard - *Love's Labours*
Cromwell - *Henry VIII*
Dauphin - *Henry V*
Davy - *Henry IV - II*
Decius - *Julius Caesar*
Demetrius - *Titus*
Doctor - *Macbeth*
Dogberry - *Much Ado*
Don John - *Much Ado*
Don Pedro - *Much Ado*
Dromio of Syracuse - *Errors*
Duke - *2 Gentlemen*
Duke - *Measure*
Duke Senior - *As You Like It*
Dumain - *Love's Labours*
Edgar - *King Lear*
Edmund - *King Lear*

Edward - *Henry VI - III*
Edward - *Richard III*
Elbow - *Measure*
Enobarbus - *Antony & Cleopatra*
Epilogue - *Henry IV - II*
Escalus - *Measure*
Exeter - *Henry V*
Feste - *12th Night*
First Player - *Hamlet*
Fisherman - *Pericles*
Flaminius - *Timon*
Flavius - *Timon*
Fluellen - *Henry V*
Fool - *King Lear*
Ford - *Merry Wives*
Friar Francis - *Much Ado*
Gadshill - *Henry IV - I*
Gardener - *Richard II*
Gardiner - *Henry VIII*
Gentleman - *Henry VIII*
Ghost - *Hamlet*
Glendower - *Henry IV - I*
Gloucester - *Henry VI - III*
Gloucester (Richard) - *Richard III*
Gower - *Henry V*
Gower - *Pericles*
Gregory - *Romeo & Juliet*
Gremio - *Shrew*
Griffith - *Henry VIII*
Grumio - *Shrew*
Hamlet - *Hamlet*
Hastings - *Henry IV - II*
Hastings - *Richard III*
Henry IV - *Henry IV - I, II*
Henry V - *Henry V*
Henry VI - *Henry VI - II, III*
Henry VIII - *Henry VIII*
Horatio - *Hamlet*
Hortensio - *Shrew*
Host - *2 Gentlemen*
Hubert - *King John*
Hume - *Henry VI - II*
Iachimo - *Cymbeline*
Iago - *Othello*
Iden - *Henry VI - II*
Jaques - *As You Like It*
John - *Henry VI - I*
Justice - *Henry IV - II*
Kent - *King Lear*
King John - *King John*
King - *Love's Labours*
Launce - *2 Gentlemen*
LeBeau - *As You Like It*
Leontes - *Winter's Tale*
Lewis - *King John*
Longaville - *Love's Labours*
Lord - *As You Like It*
Lord - *Cymbeline*
Lord - *Shrew*
Lord Say - *Henry VI - II*

Lovell - *Henry VIII*
Lucio - *Measure*
Lucullus - *Timon*
Lysimachus - *Pericles*
Macbeth - *Macbeth*
Macduff - *Macbeth*
Malcolm - *Macbeth*
Malvolio - *12th Night*
Marcus - *Titus*
Marullus - *Julius Caesar*
Melun - *King John*
Menas - *Antony & Cleopatra*
Messenger - *Henry VI - I*
Messenger - *Henry VI - III*
Messenger - *Much Ado*
Michael Williams - *Henry V*
Montjoy - *Henry V*
Morocco - *Merchant*
Mortimer - *Henry IV - I*
Morton - *Henry IV - II*
Mowbray - *Henry IV - II*
Mowbray - *Richard II*
Murderer - *Richard III*
Nestor - *Troilus & Cressida*
Nicanor - *Coriolanus*
Norfolk - *Henry VIII*
Northumberland - *Henry IV - II*
Nym - *Henry V*
Oberon - *Midsummer*
Old Talbot - *Henry VI - I*
Oliver - *As You Like It*
Orleans - *Henry V*
Orsino - *12th Night*
Osric - *Hamlet*
Othello - *Othello*
Painter - *Timon*
Palamon - *2 Noble Kinsmen*
Pandar - *Pericles*
Pandarus - *Troilus & Cressida*
Pandulph - *King John*
Paris - *Troilus & Cressida*
Parolles - *All's Well*
Pembroke - *King John*
Pericles - *Pericles*
Petruchio - *Shrew*
Philip the Bastard - *King John*
Pirithous - *2 Noble Kinsmen*
Pisanio - *Cymbeline*
Pistol - *Henry IV - II*
Pistol - *Henry V*
Player King - *Hamlet*
Poet - *Timon*
Polixenes - *Winter's Tale*
Pompey - *Measure*
Porter - *Macbeth*
Porter's Man - *Henry VIII*
Prologue - *Henry VIII*
Proteus - *2 Gentlemen*
Provost - *Measure*
Quickly - *Henry IV - II*

Quickly - *Henry V*
Richard - *Henry VI - III*
Richard II - *Richard II*
Richard III - *Richard III*
Richmond - *Richard III*
Rivers - *Richard III*
Robert - *King John*
Roderigo - *Othello*
Rosencrantz/Guildenstern - *Hamlet*
Ross - *Macbeth*
Rumour - *Henry IV - II*
Salanio - *Merchant*
Salarino - *Merchant*
Salisbury - *King John*
Sampson - *Romeo & Juliet*
Sands - *Henry VIII*
Scroop - *Richard II*
Sebastian - *Tempest*
Sempronius - *Timon*
Servant - *Coriolanus*
Servant - *Romeo & Juliet*
Servant - *Shrew*
Servant - *Timon*
Servant - *Troilus & Cressida*
Shallow - *Henry IV - II*
Shepherd - *Winter's Tale*
Sicinius - *Coriolanus*
Sly - *Shrew*
Soldier - *Henry V*
Speed - *2 Gentlemen*
Stephano - *Tempest*
Suffolk - *Henry VI - I*
Suffolk - *Henry VI - II*
Suffolk - *Henry VIII*
Surrey - *Henry VIII*
Surveyor - *Henry VIII*
Talbot - *Henry VI - I*
Thersites - *Troilus & Cressida*
Theseus - *Midsummer*
Timon - *Timon*
Titus - *Titus*
Toby - *12th Night*
Touchstone - *As You Like It*
Tranio - *Shrew*
Trinculo - *Tempest*
Tybalt - *Romeo & Juliet*
Tyrrel - *Richard III*
Ulysses - *Troilus & Cressida*
Valentine - *2 Gentlemen*
Warwick - *Henry IV - II*
Warwick - *Henry VI - III*
Warwick/York - *Henry VI - I*
Westmoreland - *Henry IV - II*
Wolsey - *Henry VIII*
Wooer - *2 Noble Kinsmen*
Worcester - *Henry IV - I*
York - *Henry VI - II, III*

WOMEN: ADULT *(ages 25 - 45)*

Adriana - *Comedy of Errors*
Alice - *Henry V*
[Archidamus] - *Winter's Tale*
[Ariel] - *Tempest*
Bawd - *Pericles*
Beatrice - *Much Ado*
Calpurnia - *Julius Caesar*
[Camillo] - *Winter's Tale*
[Chorus] - *Henry V*
[Cleomenes/Dion] - *Winter's Tale*
Cleopatra - *Antony & Cleopatra*
Constance - *King John*
Courtesan - *Comedy of Errors*
Cressida - *Troilus & Cressida*
Dionyzia - *Pericles*
[Doctor] - *2 Noble Kinsmen*
Doll - *Henry IV - II*
Elinor - *King John*
Emilia - *Othello*
[Feste] - *12th Night*
[Fool] - *King Lear*
Gentlewoman - *Macbeth*
Helen - *Troilus & Cressida*
Hermione - *Winter's Tale*
[Jailer] - *2 Noble Kinsmen*
Jailer's Daughter - *2 Noble Kinsmen*
Julia - *2 Gentlemen*
Katharina - *Shrew*
Lady Capulet - *Romeo & Juliet*
Lady Grey - *Henry VI - III*
Lady Macbeth - *Macbeth*
Lucetta - *2 Gentlemen*
Luciana - *Comedy of Errors*
Margaret - *Henry VI - I*
Margaret - *Much Ado*
Maria - *12th Night*
[Messenger] - *Much Ado*
Mistress Quickly - *Henry IV - I*
Mistress Quickly - *Henry IV - II*
Mistress Quickly - *Merry Wives*
Mrs. Ford - *Merry Wives*
Mrs. Page - *Merry Wives*
Old Lady - *Henry VIII*
Olivia - *12th Night*
[Page] - *Shrew*
Paulina - *Winter's Tale*
[Pirithous] - *2 Noble Kinsmen*
Player Queen - *Hamlet*
Portia - *Julius Caesar*
[Prologue] - *Henry VIII*
Queen Katharine - *Henry VIII*
Queen Margaret - *Henry VI - II, III*
Queen - *Richard II*
Regan - *King Lear*
[Servant] - *Shrew*
[Servant] - *Troilus & Cressida*
Silvia - *2 Gentlemen*
[Speed] - *2 Gentlemen*

Tamora - *Titus*
Titania - *Midsummer*
Valeria - *Coriolanus*
Virgilia - *Coriolanus*

WOMEN: OLDER/CHARACTER

Duchess of Gloucester-*Henry VI-II*
Duchess of Gloucester - *Richard II*
Duchess of York - *Richard II*
Duchess of York - *Richard III*
[Jailer] - *2 Noble Kinsmen*
Nurse - *Romeo & Juliet*
Queen Elizabeth - *Richard III*
Queen Margaret - *Richard III*
Volumnia - *Coriolanus*
Witches - *Macbeth*

MEN: OLDER/CHARACTER

Adam - *As You Like It*
Belarius - *Cymbeline*
Brabantio - *Othello*
Caesar - *Julius Caesar*
Cranmer - *Henry VIII*
Egeus - *Midsummer*
Flavius - *Timon*
Falstaff - *Henry IV - I, II*
Falstaff - *Merry Wives*
Father - *Henry VI - III*
Fr. Laurence - *Romeo & Juliet*
France - *All's Well*
France - *Henry V*
Gaunt - *Richard II*
Gloucester - *Henry VI - II*
Gloucester - *King Lear*
Gobbo - *Merchant*
Jailer - *2 Noble Kinsmen*
Lafeu - *All's Well*
Lear - *King Lear*
Leonato - *Much Ado*
Menenius - *Coriolanus*
More - *Sir Thomas More*
Polonius - *Hamlet*
Prospero - *Tempest*
Shepherd - *Henry VI - I*
Shylock - *Merchant*
York - *Richard II*

INDEX: Specialty Scenes

(The characters in parentheses appear in the scene but are not required to sing or fence.)

SINGERS

AMIENS/(Jaques) .... *As You Like It* 3:15 65
ARIEL/(Prospero, etc.) .... *Tempest* .... 6:21 ... 130
AUTOLYCUS/(Clown) .... *Winter's Tale* 6:45 87
DESDEMONA/(Emilia) ... *Othello* 4:48 91
FESTE/(Toby/Andrew) ... *Twelfth Night* .... 3:45 ... 120
FESTE/(Orsino/Viola) .... *Twelfth Night* .... 6:21 ... 121
JAILER'S DAUGHTER .... *Two Noble Kinsmen* 1:18 6
JAILER'S DAUGHTER .... *Two Noble Kinsmen* 6:48 6
OPHELIA .... *Hamlet* 3:45 9
OPHELIA/(Gertrude, etc.) . *Hamlet* .... 11:18 ... 124
PANDARUS/(Paris/Helen) *Troilus & Cressida* .... 6:15 ... 119
PORTIA/(Bassanio) .... *Merchant of Venice* .... 9:21 ... 100
PROTEUS/(Host, etc.) ..... *Two Gentlemen* .... 5:36 ... 131

FENCERS

ARCITE/PALAMON ..... *Two Noble Kinsmen* 6:33 86
ARCITE/PALAMON ..... *Two Noble Kinsmen* 25:00 86
CHARLES/JOAN .... *Henry VI, Part I* 3:43 96
MACBETH/MACDUFF ... *Macbeth* 1:42 76
PRINCE HAL/HOTSPUR . *Henry IV, Part I* 2:03 71
ROMEO/MERCUTIO/
TYBALT/(Benvolio) ...... *Romeo & Juliet* .... 7:06 ... 130

THE PLAYS OF SHAKESPEARE

Comedies

All's Well That Ends Well
As You Like It
The Comedy of Errors
Love's Labours Lost
Measure for Measure
The Merchant of Venice
The Merry Wives of Windsor
A Midsummer Night's Dream
Much Ado About Nothing
The Taming of the Shrew
Twelfth Night
The Two Gentlemen of Verona

Tragedies

Antony and Cleopatra
Coriolanus
Hamlet
Julius Caesar
King Lear
Macbeth
Othello
Romeo and Juliet
Timon of Athens
Titus Andronicus
Troilus and Cressida

Histories

King Henry IV, Part I
King Henry IV, Part II
King Henry V
King Henry VI, Part I
King Henry VI, Part II
King Henry VI, Part III
King Henry VIII
King John
King Richard II
King Richard III
Sir Thomas More*

Romances

Cymbeline
Pericles
The Tempest
The Two Noble Kinsmen**
The Winter's Tale

* only a fragment exists
** possibly a collaboration
between Shakespeare and
John Fletcher